ABUNDANT SOUL

DAILY MEDITATIONS FOR A FLOURISHING LIFE

DR. RICHELLE HOEKSTRA-ANDERSON

KI PRODUCTIONS

Abundant Soul
Daily Meditations for a Flourishing Life

Copyright © 2025 by Richelle Hoekstra-Anderson
Paperback ISBN: 978-1-961605-54-1

KI Productions
Noblesville, IN

Unless indicated otherwise, all Holy Scripture quotations are taken from the Holy Bible, New International Version, NIV Copyright 1984.

KI PRODUCTIONS
Where every story matters

This book is lovingly dedicated to the memory of my parents,

Dick and Betty Hoekstra.

Your selfless love, unending encouragement, and unwavering belief in me are the roots of who I am today. Thank you for laying the foundation of faith, resilience, and unconditional love that shaped my life. Your legacy continues to bloom through these pages.

CONTENTS

PART THREE
TEND YOUR SOUL FOR A THRIVING LIFE GARDEN

PART FOUR
PESTS AND WEEDS—OVERCOME SPIRITUAL HINDRANCES

PART FIVE
FLOURISH IN ALL SEASONS AND LEAVE A LEGACY

Dear Beautiful Soul,

As you open these pages, I want you to hold onto a beautiful truth:

You are a rose in the eyes of God.

Carefully planted, deeply loved, and intentionally tended, you are not here by accident. No matter where you've been, what you've faced, or how you see yourself, the Master Gardener—God Himself—sees your beauty, your strength, and your sacred potential.

Your life is a garden. Some seasons are full of sunshine and blossoms, while others bring storms, pruning, or dry, barren ground. But through every season, God is always at work. He knows when your soul needs gentle rain, when your roots need to grow deeper to withstand the winds of hardship, and when to lovingly prune what no longer serves your growth—because He sees the masterpiece He is creating in you.

A rose does not question the Gardener's hands; it simply trusts that it is being shaped into something breathtaking.

That's the heart behind this book—and the title *Abundant Soul: Daily Meditations for a Flourishing Life*. Jesus said, "I came that they may have life, and have it abundantly" (John 10:10). He doesn't want you merely surviving—He wants you flourishing. He invites you into a life rooted in His love and overflowing with peace, joy, and purpose. A life that reflects His beauty and goodness, from the inside out.

This book was birthed from years of soul-deep conversations, life lessons, and sacred moments I've shared with clients throughout my 35-year journey as a clinical psychologist and life coach. It also grew out of my *Abundant Mindset with Dr. Richelle* Facebook group, where I've offered daily encouragement and inspiration since 2020. Many of these meditations began as quiet seeds planted there—words spoken in season that met hearts right where they were.

As you read these meditations, I invite you to slow down. Let them wash over you.

Savor the truth. Ponder the words. Read not for more information, but for transformation. These are not just ideas—they are seeds of truth meant to be absorbed by the soul and rooted deep within. And when truth takes root, it brings lasting change.

These meditations are shaped by what I've learned walking alongside others through valleys and breakthroughs, grief and growth. They're inspired by the questions, prayers, and struggles I've heard from women longing to live not just faithfully—but fully. And they are grounded in one unchanging truth: *Jesus calls you to life—and life more abundantly.*

Abundant Soul was lovingly created to guide you through 67 days of growth, renewal, and transformation. Recent research suggests it takes about 65 to 67 days to form a lasting habit. My heart's desire is to help you cultivate the life-giving rhythm of soul care—of showing up each day with intention, grace, and a willingness to let God nourish, heal, and restore the places within you that long to flourish.

These daily meditations are your sacred invitation to receive more of the abundant life Jesus promised—not just in your outer circumstances, but deep within. Through quiet reflection, honest prayer, and an ever-growing awareness of God's loving presence, you'll begin to live from a place of greater wholeness, resilience, and joy.

Each day ends with two gentle yet powerful invitations: a **declaration to speak aloud**, and **reflection questions** to guide your heart.

Why the declaration? Because your voice matters. When you speak God's truth out loud, something shifts. Neuroscience confirms what Scripture has long shown—repetition shapes the brain. The more you speak truth, the more it becomes part of your inner narrative. Your brain believes your own voice more than any other. So when you declare truth —especially when you don't *feel* it yet—you're helping to rewire your thoughts, strengthen your spirit, and align your mind with God's Word. You're planting seeds that grow into peace, confidence, and freedom.

Then comes **reflection**. Let the questions make space for a real, honest conversation between you and God. Write down your thoughts, prayers, and even your questions or doubts. This is where soul care deepens— not in rushing, but in showing up fully. It doesn't need to be perfect. It just needs to be true. As you sit with these questions, allow yourself to write out what first comes to mind.

It is my heartfelt prayer that these daily meditations draw you closer to God, help you see yourself through His eyes, and anchor your heart in the truth that you are deeply cherished. You may notice certain truths repeated throughout—this isn't by accident. Repetition waters the roots of your soul, helping you absorb and embody the truth of your worth, your identity, and your sacred value in God's eyes.

And as you begin to love yourself the way God already loves you, you will reflect His beauty in the world around you—in the unique and irreplaceable way only *you* can. You'll step more fully into the flourishing life He's always intended for you.

Just like a rose doesn't bloom overnight, your emotional and spiritual growth will unfold slowly, intentionally, and with grace. Trust the process. God is tending to you.

A rose is more than a flower—it's a symbol of love, resilience, and beauty. It stands tall even with thorns, reminding us that joy and struggle often grow side by side. And just like the rose's fragrance lingers long after it's gone, so too will the legacy of a life rooted in God's love.

So step into this sacred garden with me. Let the Master Gardener care for your soul, remove the weeds of doubt, and nourish you with His presence. And with each passing day, may you come to believe, more deeply than ever before, that you are wonderfully made, wholly loved, and blooming exactly as He intended.

With love,

Dr. Richelle

ACKNOWLEDGMENTS

To **Marya Sherron**—thank you for your beautiful insight, wisdom, and skill. You caught the vision of what this book means to me and helped me shape it with care and purpose. Your support and encouragement have been a tremendous gift.

To **Elise Hartman**—thank you for helping me organize years of Facebook reflections into thoughtful categories. Your gift for structure and detail brought clarity and helped make this book a reality.

To **Diane Bray**—thank you for your keen eye for detail and thoughtful edits that helped make the message clearer. Your contribution strengthened the heart of this book and brought a beautiful polish to each page.

To my dear friends, **Cyndi Holder, Ann Schlice, and Diane O'Connor**—thank you for being my cheerleaders, prayer partners, and encouragers. Your belief in me and in the power of these words has meant more than you know.

To my daughters, **Hillary Driessen and Bethany Morrisson**—you are two of my greatest joys. You inspire me daily. May this book be a reflection of the faith and love I hope to leave in you and in all who come after you.

To my precious grandsons, **Ronin Driessen**, **Leo Morrison**, and all my future grandchildren—this book holds the legacy of grace I long to sow into your hearts. May you grow up rooted in truth, covered in prayer, and confident in your God-given worth.

To my husband, **John Anderson**—thank you for your steady love, faithful support, and the way you have walked beside me in every season. Your encouragement has been a quiet strength through this entire writing journey.

To **Jesus**—thank You for showing me over and over again Your faithfulness and amazing grace. Your love is the heartbeat behind every page.

"May these words of my mouth and this meditation of my heart be pleasing in your sight, Lord, my Rock and my Redeemer."
Psalm 19:14

PART ONE
THE MASTER GARDENER - FAITHFUL, LOVING AND TRUE

Every thriving garden begins with the care of someone who knows what it needs to grow. Before anything else, your heart—your soul—must be entrusted to the One who created it.

God is the Master Gardener of your life. He is intentional in His design, faithful in His care, and relentless in His love for you. He sees the beauty that's still unfolding, the growth happening beneath the surface, and the strength being formed in quiet, hidden places. With gentle hands, He prunes, waters, and tends your soul—not with haste, but with patience and deep compassion.

This is your sacred invitation—not to strive, but to *abide*.

This book isn't a checklist or a challenge—it's a gentle rhythm of slowing down and tending to your soul. It's about returning to the God who sees you, knows you, and wants to walk with you—not just in the big moments, but in the ordinary ones too.

Over the next few days, you'll be invited to sit with foundational truths:

God is always with you.
His love for you is unconditional and unshakable.

Your identity is rooted in Him—not in your past, your performance, or your pain.
The Spirit of God lives in you and empowers you to live freely and fully.
Even in life's valleys, you are held, strengthened, and never forgotten.
What you believe about God will shape everything else.

So as you enter this first part of the journey, you're not being asked to do anything grand. Just this:

Pause.

Be still.

Let God meet you right where you are. This is where soul care begins—with Immanuel, **God with you**.

Step Into Abundance
Day 1

*"The thief comes only to steal and kill and destroy; I have come
that they may have life, and have it to the full."*
John 10:10

WELCOME TO THIS SACRED SPACE—A place where you can
breathe, rest, and reconnect with the One who created you. This
journey isn't about doing more. It's about becoming more rooted in
what already matters most—God's presence, His love, and the care of
your soul.

As you begin these 67 days of reflection, I invite you to pause. Set aside
the rush. Let go of the pressure to perform or prove. This is your invitation to slow down and sit with God—*and with yourself.*

God never meant for you to just get by. He didn't create you for survival
mode or surface-level success. He created you for *abundance*—a life that
flows from connection with Him. One rooted in peace, purpose, joy,
and rest. He walks with you not just on the mountaintops but in the
valleys too. And He meets you exactly where you are—not when you
have it all together, but right now.

What if abundance isn't something you strive for... but something you *receive*? Imagine a life that's less rushed and more rooted. One where your worth isn't measured by how much you get done, but by how deeply you stay connected—to God, to your own soul, and to the people who matter most. A life aligned with His rhythm of grace.

The world teaches you to chase happiness. But joy—the kind that lasts —begins from the inside out. It grows slowly, like fruit on a tree, nourished by truth, gratitude, and a daily choice to abide in Jesus. You don't have to force joy, peace, or purpose. You only need to *remain* in Him. He does the transforming.

You will have hard days. That's part of the journey. But even in those moments, God is at work. Even in the quiet, He is moving. And even when you can't see the full picture, He's still writing your story.

So today, before you move on to the next thing, ask yourself gently:

What would it look like to truly live abundantly—from the inside out?

Not perfectly. Not all at once. But slowly, intentionally. By showing up with God. By tending to your heart. By trusting that even here, even now—He is with you. This is the beginning of a beautiful journey— one of grace, growth, and soul-deep care. Let today be your *yes* to the life Jesus came to give:

Full. Flourishing. Abundant.

DECLARATION

I receive the abundant life Jesus came to give me. Today, I will tend to my soul and trust that God is at work within me.

Reflection

In what areas of your life do you feel like you're just getting by instead of living fully?

What would it look like to make space for soul care in this season?

You Are Invited to Soul-Care

Day 2

"But blessed is the one who trusts in the Lord, whose confidence is in Him. They will be like a tree planted by the water that sends out its roots by the stream. It does not fear when heat comes; its leaves are always green."
Jeremiah 17:7–8

Take a deep breath, friend. You're in the right place.

This isn't just another meditation—it's the beginning of something sacred. A moment to pause, to breathe, and to care for one of the most important parts of your life: your soul.

There's a saying I love:

"The best time to plant a tree was 20 years ago. The second-best time is today." And I believe the same is true for learning how to take care of your soul. Maybe the best time was long ago... but the second-best time? It's right now.

You might be wondering, *"But how do I even begin?"*

Let me share a moment from my own story. I remember when everything shifted for me. I was in the thick of my cancer battle—my body

7

and mind worn down by the harsh realities of chemo. I felt sick, weak, and afraid. The doctors gave me my "odds of survival," and none of the numbers felt reassuring. But as I stared down my mortality, one truth became clear:

My life was—and always had been—in God's hands.

"For in Him we live and move and have our being."
Acts 17:28 (KJV)

I won't sugarcoat it. In those moments, even prayer felt hard. My body was drained, my emotions raw. But still, I sensed His presence. And that's when I realized—without even knowing it, I had actually been tending to my soul for years.

Those quiet moments in Scripture...

The whispered prayers...

The worship through tears...

They were the roots that held me steady when the storm came.

I didn't know if I would survive cancer...

But I knew I wouldn't face it alone.

That truth changed everything.

That season taught me something powerful: caring for my soul was just as vital as caring for my body. Healing wasn't only about medicine. It meant nurturing my heart, mind, relationships—my whole self. So I leaned in deeper and anchored myself in the rich soil of God's love.

And that, dear one, is what soul care is really about.

It's slowing down long enough to pay attention to what matters most.

It's strengthening your soul before the storm arrives.

It's building a life so deeply rooted in God's love that no matter what comes, you remain steady and secure.

I don't know what you're feeling today.

Maybe you're celebrating. Maybe you're longing for peace.

Maybe you need healing, rest, or simply space to breathe.

Or maybe you're just trying to make it through.

Whatever it is, hear this:

You are not alone.

This is your invitation to begin again.

To care for your soul like never before.

To dig deep.

To plant truth.

To let something beautiful grow.

No matter where you've been or how long it's taken to prioritize your soul, it's never too late.

The next best time to start is right now.

So take a deep breath... and let's begin.

DECLARATION

I choose to slow down and tend to my soul—rooted in God's love, steady in His presence.

Reflection

What part of your soul has been feeling neglected or in need of extra care lately?

What would it look like to slow down and let your roots grow deeper in God's love this week?

Nurture Your Mind, Body and Spirit Through Soul-Care

Day 3

"Love the Lord your God with all your heart and with all your
soul and with all your mind and with all your strength. The
second is this: 'Love your neighbor as yourself.' There is no
commandment greater than these."
Mark 12:30–31

SELF-CARE ISN'T JUST a trendy idea—it's a foundational part of soul-care. It's about honoring your mind, body, and spirit so you can live fully and love others from a place of wholeness, not weariness.

God designed you as an integrated being—body, soul, and spirit. When one part is neglected, the others feel the strain. That's why soul-care isn't just spiritual; it's practical. It looks like getting enough rest, nourishing your body, guarding your thoughts, setting boundaries, and creating space for stillness. It's learning to listen to your needs instead of ignoring them for the sake of productivity or approval.

It's all too easy to keep saying "yes," to give and give until there's nothing left. We pour ourselves out in caregiving, ministry, work, or relationships—often while quietly running on empty. But here's the truth: you weren't created to live depleted.

If you don't take time to care for yourself, you'll eventually have nothing left to offer. You cannot pour from an empty cup—and God never asked you to.

Self-care isn't selfish—and it's not a luxury. It's a holy rhythm of honoring the life God entrusted to you. When you pause to rest, to breathe, to nourish your body, to renew your mind—you're participating in sacred work. You're aligning your life with the truth that your worth doesn't come from what you do, but from whose you are.

Choosing to nurture yourself is choosing to live intentionally. You're not just getting by—you're investing in your capacity to live, love, and lead well. You're allowing God's peace to take root, His grace to shape your pace, and His presence to renew your strength.

So the next time you feel guilty for resting or saying no, remember this:

You are not a machine. You are a beloved child of God.

Caring for yourself is part of honoring Him.

DECLARATION

I choose to care for my whole self—body, soul, and spirit—as an act of worship and wisdom.

Reflection

Where in your life have you been running on empty—and what would it look like to refill your cup this week?

What's one belief or mindset that's been keeping you from making space for your own care—and how might you begin to shift it?

What You Believe About God Changes Everything

Day 4

"*But when the kindness and love of God our Savior appeared, He saved us, not because of righteous things we had done, but because of His mercy. He saved us through the washing of rebirth and renewal by the Holy Spirit.*"
Titus 3:4–5

"*What comes into our minds when we think about God is the most important thing about us.*"
A.W. Tozer

What comes to mind when you think of God?

Pause for a moment and really ask yourself: *What do I believe about Him?* Because what you believe about God shapes everything—how you see yourself, how you navigate life, and where you place your hope.

If you don't believe in God at all, life becomes about squeezing as much pleasure as you can out of your short time here. But eventually, that emptiness creeps in, whispering, *Is this really all there is?*

If you believe there is a God, but He's distant or unknowable, you may find yourself wandering—searching for love, purpose, and security in places that will never truly satisfy.

If you believe God is angry with you, disappointed, or has given up on you, you may hide in shame—hoping that somehow being "good enough" will make things right. But the weight of trying to earn love and forgiveness is exhausting. And you were never meant to carry that weight.

But oh, friend, if you believe that Jesus is God in the flesh—who came to rescue, redeem, and restore you—then *everything* changes.

You'll begin to live knowing you are fully loved, fully accepted, just as you are.

You'll believe that your life has meaning and purpose because you were uniquely created by God Himself.

You'll embrace the truth that you were made for an abundant life now and an eternal home with Him later.

You'll find deep joy in discovering who He is, how He provides for you, and how He walks with you through every high and low.

And in your darkest days—when your heart is breaking, when the weight of the world feels unbearable, when loss, fear, or regret try to consume you—you will not be alone. Because the One who holds the stars in place holds you too.

Let me remind you of what God thinks when He looks at you:

My child, I love you more than you can imagine. I knew you could never reach perfection on your own, and that's why I sent My Son, Jesus, to take your place. You don't have to earn my love—it is already yours. When I look at you, I see you covered by the perfection of Jesus. Your sins are forgiven. You are Mine. My Spirit is within you, and I will walk with you every step of the way. Take my hand, and let's walk this journey together.

What a beautiful, breathtaking truth.

So when the days are hard and your heart aches, come back to these words. Let them settle deep in your soul. When you're waiting for answers, waiting for healing, waiting for a breakthrough—remember, His presence is your peace.

When the choices of someone you love steal your joy—remember, He is your source of joy. When painful memories try to drag you back into the valley—remember, He is the way through. You are never alone, no matter how lonely you feel.

He is with you, always.

And that, dear one, is the sweetest truth of all.

DECLARATION

I am fully loved and accepted by God—purely by His grace through Jesus.

Reflection

When you think about God, what comes to mind? Does that picture align with who He really is?

How would your day-to-day life shift if you truly believed you are fully loved and fully accepted by God?

Embrace the Freedom of Unconditional Love

Day 5

"My old self has been crucified with Christ. It is no longer I who live, but Christ lives in me. So I live in this earthly body by trusting in the Son of God, who loved me and gave himself for me."
Galatians 2:20 (NLT)

HERE'S a life-changing truth to hold onto: **God loves you unconditionally.**

Let that sink in for a moment.

You don't have to strive for God's approval—you already have it. Jesus lived the perfect life precisely because you can't.

Every unkind word, hidden motive, anxious thought, or missed mark in your life—Jesus took it all to the cross. He didn't give His life for you because you had it all together. He gave His life *so* you could be with Him—whole, free, and fully known.

This is where soul-care begins. Not with what you can do for God, but with what He's already done for you. The abundant life He promises isn't about striving harder—it's about receiving with a grateful heart.

You were created for a close, abiding connection with God. And the more you recognize that His Spirit now lives in you, the more grounded and whole you become. Your relationships grow richer. Your self-worth becomes rooted in truth. You begin to love more freely, give more generously, and walk through life with greater peace.

So take a deep breath today.

Inhale His grace.

Exhale the pressure.

Let His peace settle over you like a gentle covering.

He is with you.

He is in you.

And you are fully, completely, unconditionally loved.

DECLARATION

Christ lives in me, and I am fully loved, accepted, and free—not because I am perfect, but because He is.

Reflection

How would your life change if you truly believed you are fully loved—
just as you are?

What does it look like to live today with Christ living in you?

You Are Rooted in God's Love
Day 6

"...And I pray that you, being rooted and established in love, may have power, together with all the Lord's holy people, to grasp how wide and long and high and deep is the love of Christ, and to know this love that surpasses knowledge—that you may be filled to the measure of all the fullness of God."
Ephesians 3:17–19

YESTERDAY, we paused to reflect on the breathtaking truth of God's unconditional love for you. Today, we return to that same truth—because it bears repeating. Again and again.

Why? Because this truth is foundational. It must be drilled deep into the soil of your heart—until it becomes the rich root system from which your identity, peace, and purpose grow. So let's say it again, slowly:

God loves me.

Not in theory. Not in general. God loves *you*—personally, deeply, fully. And here's something else your heart needs to hear today: God doesn't just love you... He *likes* you.

Yes, the Creator of the universe delights in the very things that make you *you*. He enjoys the way you smile, the way you show up for others, the way your gifts, talents, and personality shine light into the world. You were handcrafted with intention—and He doesn't just tolerate your uniqueness, He *cherishes* it.

He sees you completely—every strength, every weakness, every scar—and still chooses you with joy. His love doesn't shrink back on your hard days. It doesn't hinge on your performance. It is steady, safe, and unwavering. When this kind of love sinks deep into your soul, it changes everything.

It calms your fears. It heals your shame. It silences the inner critic. It empowers you to stop striving and start living from a place of peace and security. You don't have to earn what has already been lavished upon you. You are rooted in His love. And when you live from that rooted place, you become grounded and resilient. You become a vessel of love, grace, and strength—free to be fully and joyfully yourself.

So pause again.

Open your heart. Receive the love that holds nothing back. Let it wash over every doubt and insecurity. Let it soak into the places that still wonder if you're enough. Because you are.

You are loved. You are liked.

And you are growing into the beautiful, flourishing soul God designed you to be.

DECLARATION

God loves me—and He delights in who I am. I am rooted, secure, and free to be joyfully me.

Reflection

Where in your life do you still struggle to believe that God not only loves you, but truly *likes* you?

How might your confidence, relationships, or self-talk shift if you embraced the truth that you are fully known, fully loved, and joyfully delighted in by your Creator?

Immanuel: God Is With You, Always

Day 7

"Where can I go from your Spirit? Where can I flee from your presence? If I go up to the heavens, you are there; if I make my bed in the depths, you are there. If I rise on the wings of the dawn, if I settle on the far side of the sea, even there your hand will guide me, your right hand will hold me fast."
Psalm 139:7–10

THE NAME *IMMANUEL* means "God with us," and it's more than a name—it's a truth that changes everything.

You might find yourself chasing after the presence of God, as if it's something you have to earn or go out and find. But as spiritual writer Richard Rohr so beautifully said, "We cannot attain the presence of God because we're already totally in the presence of God. What's absent is awareness."

God is with you in *every moment*—the quiet, the chaotic, the sacred, and the ordinary. When you wake up. When you pour your morning coffee. When you pack lunches or scroll your phone. When you sit in traffic or wait for test results. When you fold laundry, answer emails, hold tears, or hold hands. In every one of these moments—He is with you.

Recognizing His nearness isn't about adding one more thing to your to-do list. It's about gently shifting your awareness to the One who is already there. He's not waiting for your next devotional time to show up —He's already walking with you through your day.

When you become more aware of His presence, something changes. Your anxiety quiets. Your shoulders drop. Your soul exhales. Because deep down, you remember—you are not alone. God, your faithful Companion and Helper, is closer than your next breath.

Take time today to pause, breathe, and welcome Him. He is already near, but when you invite Him into your thoughts, your tasks, and your emotions, your perspective begins to shift. His peace enters in. His grace fills the space.

You don't need to perform, impress, or pretend. You can simply be— loved, seen, and held by a God who delights in walking with you.

DECLARATION

God is with me in every moment. I am never alone. His presence surrounds, sustains, and strengthens me—always.

Reflection

In what everyday moments do you most need to be reminded of God's presence?

How can you intentionally become more aware of God walking with you throughout your day?

Live Beyond What You Can Imagine

Day 8

"Now to Him who is able to do exceedingly abundantly above all that we ask or think, according to the power that works in us..."
Ephesians 3:20 (NKJV)

There is no limit to what God can do in your life.

LET ME SAY IT AGAIN...

There is no limit to what God can do in your life.

He is the Master Gardener, tending to you with care, and His plans for you go far beyond what you could ever imagine. Ephesians 3:20 reminds us that He is able to do "exceeding abundantly above all that we ask or think." His goodness is not scarce, nor is His love measured in small portions. He is a God of abundance, pouring out blessings, growth, and transformation in ways that surpass your wildest dreams.

A garden that flourishes in His care is not just one with a single bloom —it is overflowing with beauty, life, and fragrance. When you trust Him fully, allowing His power to work within you, your life becomes a reflection of His abundance. You will find joy sprouting in unexpected places,

31

peace taking root where worry once lived, and love spreading like vines in every direction. He is not simply tending to you so that you may survive—He is nurturing you so that you may thrive.

But abundance is not about striving; it is about surrender. A rose does not force itself to bloom; it simply opens in response to the nourishment it receives. In the same way, you do not have to work for God's love or prove your worth to receive His blessings. He desires to pour into you, to fill your life with goodness, and to bring forth a harvest of joy, hope, and purpose. Your part is to remain open, to receive, and to trust that His plans for you are far greater than what you can see.

So let your heart rest in this truth: God is working within you, cultivating something more beautiful than you could ever design on your own. Your garden—your life—was meant to flourish, to bloom abundantly, and to reflect His glory. With every petal that unfolds, may you be reminded that His love and power are at work in you, bringing forth an overflow of blessings that will touch the world around you.

DECLARATION

God is nurturing something beautiful within me, and I trust Him to bring it to full bloom in His perfect time.

Reflection

What would it look like for you to stop striving and simply surrender to God's loving care today?

In what area of your life do you need to trust that God is cultivating something far greater than you can currently see?

God in the Valleys
Day 9

"Even though I walk through the valley of the shadow of death, I will fear no evil, for you are with me."
Psalm 23:4 (ESV)

I WAS 16 years old when I had a literal mountaintop experience with God.

It happened in the breathtaking mountains of Banff, Canada, during an international Moravian Church conference for teens and young adults. One afternoon, I wandered off alone and sat near a small waterfall just beyond our lodge. As the water rushed over the rocks and the mountain air wrapped around me, something happened—something I still struggle to put into words.

I encountered God.

Not in an audible voice or visible form—but in a way that was just as real as anything I'd ever known. I felt His presence. I knew He was there. His love, His closeness, His reality—it was undeniable.

Over the years, I've had other mountaintop moments—answered prayers, miracles, and deeply personal encounters that left me forever changed. I treasure those glimpses of heaven, reminders of just how near He is. But I've come to realize something important:

It wasn't on the mountaintops that I truly came to *know* God.

It was in the valleys.

It was in the waiting. The heartbreak. The uncertainty. The suffering.

That's where I discovered His faithfulness, His wisdom, His protection, and His limitless grace.

Jesus never promised life would be easy. In fact, He warned us: *"In this world you will have trouble. But take heart! I have overcome the world."* John 16:33

The valleys will come. And when they do, they bring pain, loss, fear, and confusion.

Maybe your valley looks like illness, divorce, betrayal, grief, financial stress, addiction, or simply feeling lost. Valleys can feel endless, dark, and overwhelming.

But here's what I want you to hold onto: **You are not alone.** Jesus will never leave you—not even in your darkest moments.

He is there...

when you have nothing left to give.

when you don't know how to move forward.

when the weight of grief feels unbearable.

The valley is temporary.

Yes, you may grieve. Yes, the pain is real. But you're not meant to pitch a tent and stay there forever.

God leads you *through* the valley.

He takes your hand and guides you toward healing, restoration, and the abundant life He has for you—a life filled with love, joy, and peace (Galatians 5:22–23).

Because without the valley, you might be tempted to believe you can do life on your own.

But it's often in the surrender—when you come to the end of yourself—that you finally discover He's everything you need.

Wherever you are—on the mountaintop or deep in the valley—know this:

His hand is extended toward you.

He sees you. He hasn't forgotten you.

Take His hand.

Trust His goodness. And walk forward, knowing the One who walks with you has already overcome it all.

DECLARATION

Even in the valley, I am never alone. God is with me, guiding me through to healing and hope.

Reflection

What valley have you walked through—or are walking through—that has helped you know God more deeply?

How is God inviting you to take His hand and trust Him with your next step?

Held by the God of Peace

Day 10

"You will keep in perfect peace all who trust in you, all whose thoughts are fixed on you."
Isaiah 26:3 (NLT)

I REMEMBER it like it was yesterday.

I was curled up in a fetal position on my bed, completely wrecked by the words I had just heard. The ICU doctor's voice echoed in my mind— *"There's nothing more we can do."*

My mom's lungs were failing. Just a week earlier, she had been admitted with COVID-19. And now, just like that, I was being told she wasn't going to make it. The weight of it all crushed me.

My dad—also sick with COVID-19—had just been released from the hospital into my care the day before. And now, I was about to lose my mom. It felt like the air had been ripped from my lungs. I couldn't think. I couldn't move. I was disoriented, in disbelief, and completely helpless. From the depths of my soul, I cried out, *"God, I don't know how to do this."* And then—in the middle of my brokenness—I heard it. A whisper. Not audible, but unmistakable: *I am with you.*

In that moment, I knew the only way I was going to make it through was by clinging to Him—fixing my eyes on His love for me, His love for my family, and His promise to be my strength. And He was. In my weakness, He was strong. In my grief, He was my comfort. In the chaos, He was my peace. Moment by moment, breath by breath, I held onto Him. I whispered His name over and over— *"Jesus, please help me."* And He did.

I don't know where you are today. Maybe you're in the middle of your own devastating storm. Maybe life feels impossible. Maybe you're just barely holding on. Maybe things are good—or somewhere in between. Wherever you are, I need you to know this: **Jesus is real.** And He is as close as your next breath.

He sees your pain. He knows the ache in your heart. And when you feel like you're drowning, He is right there—reaching for you.

Jesus doesn't always calm the storm. But He always calms His child in the middle of it. He brings a peace that doesn't make sense. A peace that holds you together when everything feels like it's falling apart. A peace not tied to circumstances—but to His presence. And it is a peace like no other.

So hold onto Jesus. And know this—no matter what—**He will never, ever let go of you.** Call on Him today. Right now. He's the best friend you will ever know. And with Him by your side, you *will* weather the storm.

DECLARATION

When everything feels like it's falling apart, I will fix my thoughts on Jesus—my peace, my strength, and my steady anchor.

Reflection

Where in your day do you most need to pause and invite God's peace into your heart and mind?

When have you experienced God's peace in the middle of a storm?

Cultivate a Life That Bears Fruit

Day 11

"But blessed is the one who trusts in the Lord, whose confidence is in him. They will be like a tree planted by the water that sends out its roots by the stream. It does not fear when heat comes; its leaves are always green. It has no worries in a year of drought and never fails to bear fruit."
Jeremiah 17:7–8

WHAT'S the last thing to grow on a fruit tree? The fruit. It doesn't just appear overnight. It takes time, nourishment, and care—rich soil, deep roots, the right balance of sun and rain, protection from pests, and the careful pruning of a patient gardener.

Our lives work the same way. True growth—the kind that produces lasting, beautiful fruit—happens when we are rooted in God's love and committed to abiding in Him with our whole heart. Jesus said, *"I am the vine; you are the branches. If you remain in me and I in you, you will bear much fruit; apart from me you can do nothing."* John 15:5

The word *abide* means to remain, stay, or continue. And it's a daily choice. When you abide in Him—seeking His presence through prayer, scripture, worship, and stillness—you don't have to force peace, patience, or self-control. Those fruits begin to grow naturally, like fruit ripening in its season.

Trying to be patient, self-disciplined, or spiritually strong in your own power is exhausting. Thankfully, you don't have to. As you stay connected to the Vine—Jesus—He begins to do what only He can: soften your heart, strengthen your spirit, and transform you from the inside out.

Spiritual growth isn't always steady or easy. There are seasons when it feels like you're thriving, and others when it feels dry, distracted, or stuck. That's normal.

If spending quiet time with God has felt challenging lately, you're not alone, I've been there too. But here's what I've learned: just like a muscle, your spiritual endurance grows with time and consistency. Keep showing up. Stay rooted. Even when you don't feel it, God is working. And in the right season, you will see the fruit.

In the meantime, speak this over yourself: ***God is able to do great things through me today.***

Say it out loud. Whisper it while making coffee or during your commute. Keep repeating it—because it's absolutely true.

Maybe you've thought: *I'm not special. I'm not smart enough. I don't know enough. I'm too old. I'm too young. I'm not confident enough.*

Let me remind you— Before you were even born, He knew you. He saw you. and He had a perfect plan for you.

He isn't looking for the most polished, accomplished, or perfect person. He's not impressed by status or titles. He doesn't hold your past against you. Rather, He loves partnering with His imperfect people (i.e., you and me) to do extraordinary things.

So don't hold back. The world needs the light inside you. There are people only *you* can reach, prayers only *you* can pray, and love only *you* can give.

Be fully, wonderfully, unapologetically the person God created you to be. He will equip you for every good work—no doubt about it.

Keep abiding. Keep growing. And in due season, you will bear fruit.

DECLARATION

God is able to do great things through me today.

Reflection

In which area(s) of your life God might be asking you to stay rooted and trust Him, even if you're not seeing the fruit yet?

What's one simple way you can stay connected to God today—just as you are?

PART TWO
THE SEED—EMBRACE
GOD'S LOVE

Before anything can bloom, it must first be planted. And just like a seed holds the quiet potential for beauty and growth, so do you. You were created with intention—planted by God's own hand in the rich soil of His love.

In Part I, you were invited to discover how you are seen by the Master Gardener. Now, in Part II, you'll go deeper—into the heart of who you are and whose you are. This section is all about identity—learning to see yourself the way God sees you: cherished, chosen, and deeply loved.

When you embrace the truth of His love, the soil of your life begins to shift. Doubt gives way to faith. Insecurity gives way to confidence. And little by little, the seed begins to grow.

So settle in. Let your roots go deep. And allow God's love to shape everything that's yet to bloom.

YOU ARE ON GOD'S MIND

DAY 12

"How precious are your thoughts about me, O God. They cannot be numbered! I can't even count them; they outnumber the grains of sand! And when I wake up, you are still with me."
Psalm 139:17–18 (NLT)

Do you realize you are on God's mind—constantly? And His thoughts about you aren't filled with disappointment, frustration, or judgment. No—He looks at you with the most tender, patient, and powerful love in the world.

In His eyes, you are His beloved child, uniquely created and deeply cherished. His hands of grace and mercy are extended to you, inviting you into quiet conversation—reminding you that His love isn't something you have to earn. He already took care of that. Why? Because He wants you close—now and forever.

There will never be a moment in your life when you're not on His mind. *"Be sure of this: I am with you always, even to the end of the age."* Matthew 28:20 (NLT)

Maybe you've spent years listening to lies about your worth. Maybe you've believed love must be earned—especially from God. Or maybe you've carried shame that left you feeling unworthy, disconnected, or tired. But those lies don't define you. God's truth does.

You're invited to return to that truth—to rest in His love and let it take root in your soul. He knows you fully, and still chooses you. His arms are open, ready to meet you with compassion and grace. You don't have to earn His love. You don't need to hide. You are already loved—completely and unconditionally.

Yes, this world is broken. Jesus said you'd face trouble. But He also promised you abundant life—and gave you His Spirit to help you walk in it. Even when you feel alone, you are not.

Will there still be doubts? Yes. Will all your questions be answered? Probably not. But does God care about your pain and your struggle? Absolutely. And does He want you to live with joy, peace, and purpose? Without a doubt. He's offering you the gift of His love and abundant life—right here, right now. No strings attached. What peace and joy you'll discover as you—God's precious seed—trust the Master Gardener to grow you into the truest version of yourself.

Let His love be your foundation. It's not about having everything figured out. It's about saying *yes* to the One who holds you, believes in you, and will never stop loving you. The journey to abundance begins the moment you pause, open your heart, and receive His love.

DECLARATION

God thinks of me constantly. I am deeply loved, fully known, and never alone.

Reflection

What lie about your worth have you believed that God is asking you to let go of today?

How does it feel to know that God thinks about you—and delights in you—right now?

You Are Chosen

Day 13

*"But you are a chosen people, a royal priesthood, a holy nation,
God's special possession, that you may declare the praises of Him
who called you out of darkness into His wonderful light."*
1 Peter 2:9

On Good Friday over 2,000 years ago, Jesus endured unimaginable pain—physical torture, betrayal by His friends, the judgment of His community, and the ultimate agony: the withdrawal of His Father's presence.

He hung on a cross, paying for sins He never committed. Not because He didn't have a choice, but because He knew the only way for you to have hope for eternal life was for Him to sacrifice Himself.

Without His payment for your sins, there would be no hope for the pain you're facing today. His journey to the cross wasn't just about physical suffering—it was also about emotional anguish. His sacrifice came from a place of profound love—for you. This act declares that you are seen, valued, and never truly alone in your suffering.

Why? Because you are chosen. Plain and simple.

You are loved by a perfect God who walks with you through every painful, unjust, heartbreaking moment of your life. He understands your pain. He gets your discouragement. And He hasn't turned His back on you, even if others have.

His arms stretched wide on that cross are your eternal reminder that they are still open to you now. He invites you to place your hope in Him. That strength you need for healing—He has it, and He longs for you to receive it. Whatever is burdening your heart, bring it to the foot of the cross. He's waiting there, ready to carry it for you.

And the resurrection? It's proof that the darkness you're facing isn't the end of your story. God always has the final word. Put your hope in Jesus. His unwavering love will give you the strength to take your next step—and the one after that. He is with you. He is for you. Always and forever.

So as you move forward, keep coming back to this truth: Jesus chose you. He sees you. And He walks with you into whatever comes next.

DECLARATION

I am chosen, fully loved, and never alone.

Reflection

What burden are you carrying today that you can bring to the foot of the cross?

How does knowing you are chosen by God shift the way you see your current situation?

You Are Worthy

Day 14

"...you are precious to me. You are honored, and I love you."
Isaiah 43:4 (NLT)

THERE IS NEVER a moment when you are not worthy of love. You were created in the image of God, and that truth alone gives you lasting value. You didn't earn it, and you can't lose it.

When you rest in that reality, the pressure to prove yourself starts to fade. The need to be liked or accepted by everyone begins to loosen its grip. You realize that your worth doesn't come from others' approval—it comes from the One who made you.

Someone's love for you doesn't make you more worthy. And if someone withholds love, that doesn't make you less. Yes, rejection hurts—but it doesn't define you.

Maybe you already believe this truth. Or maybe you've been looking for someone—anyone—to affirm your value. If that's you, look no further than Jesus. In His eyes, you are a masterpiece. (Ephesians 2:10)

No matter what your past holds—failures, regrets, or wounds—you are deeply loved. If others have rejected, abused, or abandoned you, know this: Jesus never will. In Him, you are enough. You are seen. You are worthy.

And when all is said and done, it won't be the opinions of others that matter—it will be the eternal, unwavering love of your Creator, the Master Gardener. So take a deep breath. Let His love hold you. You don't have to earn it. It's a gift—no strings attached—and it will carry you through this life and into eternity.

DECLARATION

I am loved. I am enough. I am worthy—because I belong to God.

Reflection

Where in your life do you still feel like you need to prove your worth?

How would your daily choices change if you truly believed you are already enough in God's eyes?

You Are More

Day 15

"Even before he made the world, God loved us and chose us in Christ to be holy and without fault in his eyes."
Ephesians 1:4 (NLT)

You are so much more than someone's opinion of you.

Let that truth sink in. You are fearfully and wonderfully made by a loving Creator who has given you unique gifts, deep value, and sacred purpose.

Your worth isn't defined by what others think or say. It's anchored in the unchanging love and grace that God has already poured out on you. He sees you—fully known, fully loved, and chosen. Long before the world even began, He looked ahead and saw *you*, and declared you worthy in Christ.

In a world where opinions shift and expectations change constantly, you can rest in the security of God's truth. His love isn't based on your performance. His view of you doesn't rise or fall with your reputation. It is steady, eternal, and personal.

When you begin to believe this, you no longer need to chase after validation or approval. You can stop measuring your value by what others see and instead embrace your identity in Christ—secure, beloved, and enough.

That confidence frees you to live with clarity, peace, and purpose. You can walk boldly in who God created you to be, using your gifts to make a difference in the world right where you are.

And here's the beautiful part: as you step into the truth of your worth, you become a reflection of God's love to those around you. You remind others—by your presence, your kindness, and your light—that they, too, are seen and chosen by God.

So when the world tries to tell you you're not enough, pause and remember this: before anything else, God chose you. That's the truth that matters most.

And when your life draws to a close, it won't be the world's opinions that count. It will be the voice of your Creator—the One who's loved you from the very beginning—saying, *You are Mine.*

DECLARATION

I am more than others' opinions—I am known, loved, and chosen by God.

Reflection

Have you ever let someone's opinion define your worth? How did it affect the way you saw yourself?

What would change in your life if you truly believed God's view of you is the only one that matters?

YOU ARE A LIGHT
DAY 16

*"You are the light of the world. A town built on a hill cannot be
hidden... In the same way, let your light shine before others, that
they may see your good deeds and glorify your Father in heaven."*
Matthew 5:14, 16

YOU ARE a person of great value. And wherever God places you, you
carry the potential to reflect that value by bringing light to others. The
question is: *Will you show up and shine?*

Every day, you pass by people who are carrying burdens you may never
see. One of the most meaningful ways you can reflect God's love is
through simple, intentional acts of kindness:

Look someone in the eye.

Smile.

Listen more than you speak.

Offer a genuine compliment.

Say please and thank you.

Lend a helping hand.

These gestures may seem small, but small things done with great love can create ripple effects. When you lead with compassion, you open the door to hope and healing. Your presence might be the encouragement someone didn't even know they needed.

And here's the beautiful part: even on your hard days, kindness lifts *you* too. Sometimes the best way to shift a heavy mood is to step outside of yourself and help someone else.

Before you move into the rest of your day, take a moment to reflect:

How do I want to show up today? What kind of energy, love, or light do I want to bring with me?

But don't stop there.

As you extend kindness to others, don't forget to offer it to yourself. Be gentle. Be gracious. Let go of the overthinking and the endless replay of what you could've done differently—or the worry about what's still ahead. Breathe deeply. Remind yourself: *You are human.* You're growing. You're learning. You're not expected to be perfect.

So today, choose the extraordinary path of grace. Not just toward others —but toward yourself.

Shine your light—fully and freely.

DECLARATION

I am one of a kind—created with purpose, covered in grace, and called to shine God's love.

Reflection

How do you want to show up today—in your words, your attitude, your presence?

Are you being as kind to yourself as you are to others? What would it look like to give yourself a little more grace today?

YOU ARE SEEN AND KNOWN
DAY 17

"The Lord is close to the brokenhearted and saves those who are crushed in spirit."
Psalm 34:18

ARE you in a season of waiting, uncertainty, disappointment, loneliness, heartache, or deep grief?

When you're in the thick of struggle, it can feel heavy. Disorienting. Hopeless. Like things may never get better.

You're not alone in feeling that way. We all walk through hard places—no one is immune to pain in this broken world. But here's the good news: **you are not alone.**

You have a Heavenly Father who sees you, knows you by name, and loves you more deeply than you can imagine. He longs to lead you through the darkness into still waters and green pastures. He wants to restore your soul, to walk beside you, guide you, and be your closest companion. (See Psalm 23.)

So how do you keep going when your strength is gone?

You call on Him. With whatever you have left.

You don't need polished prayers or the right words. Just a willing heart. Be honest. Be raw. He already knows what you're carrying—and He's waiting for you to bring it to Him.

Jesus, I need You.

Help me. Show me what to do.

Give me courage. Help me hold on.

Heal my heart. Calm my soul.

Protect the ones I love.

Let me feel You near.

Give me peace. Take away my fear.

Comfort me.

He is near. Closer than you think. And He will never stop loving you through the valley.

DECLARATION

Even in the dark and lonely places, I am seen, loved, and never alone—God is with me.

Reflection

In what area of your life do you feel unseen or overwhelmed right now?

How might your heart shift if you believed—deep down—that God is right there with you, holding you through it all?

You Are Heard

Day 18

"Cast all your anxiety on Him because He cares for you."
1 Peter 5:7

HAVE you ever noticed how hard it can be to ask for help?

Maybe somewhere along the way, you started believing that needing help made you weak—or that something must be wrong with you if you couldn't handle everything on your own. Pride might whisper, *You've got this,* even when you're worn out and barely holding it together.

But here's the truth: you were never meant to do life alone.

You were created for connection—with others, and most importantly, with God. Yes, independence is a strength, but even the strongest hearts need support. Your need isn't a flaw—it's an invitation. God designed you with that need so you would draw near to Him.

Jesus said: "Ask, and it will be given to you; seek, and you will find; knock, and the door will be opened to you... How much more will your Father in heaven give the Holy Spirit to those who ask Him?" Luke 11:9–13

God is ready to respond. He's not distant or indifferent. He's waiting for you to ask, to trust, and to invite Him into whatever you're facing.

So let me gently ask:

What are you carrying that feels too heavy?

What's been keeping you up at night or weighing on your heart in the morning?

There is nothing too big—or too small—for God.

He knows every detail of your life. He sees what no one else sees. And He cares about all of it.

Bring Him everything—your worries, your needs, your emotions, your questions. Even your doubts. Don't hold back. Just ask.

He hears you.

He cares for you.

DECLARATION

God hears me when I call—nothing I say is too small, too messy, or too much for Him.

Reflection

What are you still trying to carry on your own that God wants you to release to Him today?

How would your day change if you truly believed God was listening to every word and holding every concern close to His heart?

You Are Safe to Feel Your Emotions

Day 19

"The righteous cry out, and the Lord hears them; He delivers them from all their troubles. The Lord is close to the brokenhearted and saves those who are crushed in spirit."
Psalm 34:17–18

IF YOU'VE RECEIVED God's generous gift of forgiveness, then you not only have eternal life—you also have the gift of His Spirit living within you. That means you're not doing life alone. You have His help, His strength, and His presence with you in every single moment.

God didn't just forgive you and leave you to figure it out. He's with you —right now—in whatever mess, emotion, or struggle you're carrying. He is your Helper, your Comforter, your Guide. He is everything you need.

Jesus said, *"I have come so that they may have life, life in its fullest measure."* (John 10:10 CJB)

That kind of full life doesn't come from striving harder or pretending everything's okay. It comes from walking with Him—honestly and fully —even when your heart feels heavy.

Here's something you may need to hear today:

Your feelings are not a problem to fix. They're an invitation to slow down and pay attention.

We live in a world that encourages you to push through, numb out, or slap on a smile. But ignoring or stuffing your emotions doesn't make them go away—it just buries them deeper.

God created your emotions. They aren't random. They're part of your beautiful design.

Even the messy or painful ones are like signals on the dashboard of your soul. They offer insight into what you're thinking, believing, or experiencing.

So when emotions rise, think of them as a gentle yellow flag saying, *"Hey, slow down. Something inside needs care."*

Try starting here:

"What am I feeling right now?"

Name the emotion. Sit with it. Don't rush past it. Don't judge it. Just breathe.

Then gently ask:

"What thought or belief came before this feeling?"

"Is it true? Or is there another perspective?"

Not every thought is true. Sometimes, the stories you tell yourself don't align with what God says about you.

This is where journaling can help. It gets the swirl of emotions out of your head and onto paper—where you can see them more clearly and offer them honestly to God.

Remember: your emotions are valid, but they don't have to lead.

They're not the driver—but they're worthy of being heard.

Tending to your emotions with grace is an act of soul care. And you're not doing it alone.

So today, pause. Breathe. Ask for help.

God is not intimidated by your sadness, fear, or frustration. He welcomes it—and He welcomes you.

You are safe to feel.

Even more, you are safe to bring those feelings to Jesus.

DECLARATION

My feelings are safe with God—He sees, hears, and lovingly walks with me through every emotion.

Reflection

What emotion have I been avoiding, stuffing down, or brushing past lately? What might it be trying to show me?

What would it look like today to sit with that feeling in God's presence and let Him meet me there?

You Are Free

Day 20

"So if the Son sets you free, you will be free indeed."
John 8:36

WHAT WOULD you do if you truly believed you were free—free from fear, worry, failure, or judgment?

Would you finally have that honest conversation? Speak up when you disagree? Say no to what keeps pulling you away from what matters most?

Would you change jobs? Take a mental health day without guilt? Start dating again? Retire? Book the vacation you keep putting off? Get that tattoo or pierce your nose? Go out to dinner or see a movie alone? Sign up for that class you've always wanted to try?

Would you stop believing the lie that it's too late or that you're too old? Would you start your own business? Do something just for you—even if no one else understands?

Maybe you'd write that book. Walk away from a toxic relationship. Hire a life coach. Stop enabling someone else's unhealthy choices. Change careers. Or finally visit that place you've dreamed of for years.

Here's the truth: **fear is a liar.**

It tries to convince you that you can't, that you shouldn't, or that something bad will happen if you do. It shackles you to imagined worst-case scenarios and keeps your world small.

But in Christ—you are already free. And that freedom isn't just a nice idea or a future goal. It's your present reality. It's your inheritance as a child of God.

You've been set free from fear, shame, and people-pleasing.

You've been set free to live boldly, love deeply, and walk confidently in the purpose God has for you.

What if today, you started living like it?

Embrace the freedom that is already yours in Christ.

DECLARATION

I am free in Christ—free to show up fully, live boldly, and walk in truth without fear.

Reflection

If fear didn't have a say, what is one bold or honest step you'd take today toward the life you feel called to live?

What lie has fear been whispering to you—and what truth from God can you replace it with?

You Are His

Day 21

"Do not fear, for I have redeemed you; I have summoned you by name; you are mine."
Isaiah 43:1

TAKE A DEEP BREATH, friend. Let this truth settle into your soul: you are seen, known, and deeply loved.

Through these daily meditation you've been on a journey—rediscovering who you are in God's eyes.

Not who the world says you are.

Not who your past mistakes try to define you as.

Not who your fears whisper you might be.

But who God says you are.

You are His masterpiece—woven together with divine purpose.

You are chosen, set apart, and called by name.

You carry His light.

You are strong, even in weakness, because His power lives in you.

You are forgiven—fully covered by grace.

You are a warrior, equipped for every battle—because He fights for you.

You are enough, because He is more than enough.

And through it all, God gently whispers: **You are Mine.**

So today, don't just read these words—receive them.

Let them soak in like a sunrise breaking through the dark.

No more shrinking back. No more questioning your worth.

No more letting fear or doubt define your identity.

You are His. And that truth changes everything.

Walk forward boldly—not because you have it all figured out, but because the One who holds the universe also holds you.

And in Him, you can confidently declare:

I am loved. I am chosen. I am enough. I am His.

Let that be the truth you carry into today—and every day ahead.

DECLARATION

I am who God says I am—loved, chosen, and His masterpiece.

Reflection

Which of the truths above do you most need to believe today?

What would shift in your life if you fully embraced your identity in Christ today?

PART THREE
TEND YOUR SOUL FOR A THRIVING LIFE GARDEN

If you've ever tried to grow a garden, you know it doesn't just happen on its own. It takes intention. Consistency. A little mess. And a lot of grace.

The same is true for your soul.

This next section is all about learning to care for your inner life in ways that help you thrive—not just survive. Like a garden, your soul needs tending. That means pulling out the weeds of old mindsets, replacing lies with God's truth, watering your spirit with grace, and making space for rest and stillness in God's presence.

But it's not only about reflection. This part of the journey will also give you **practical tools and gentle mindset shifts** to help you create the kind of daily rhythms that lead to a truly flourishing life.

We'll talk about how to renew your thoughts, shift emotional patterns, and care for your heart in real, tangible ways—because transformation happens when truth meets action.

Whether you're feeling depleted or just ready to grow deeper, this is your invitation to slow down, be honest with yourself, and let God lovingly shape your thoughts, emotions, and daily choices.

You were made to flourish—from the inside out.

Let's tend the soil of your soul, together.

Daily Practices for a Thriving Soul

Day 22

"Dear friend, I pray that you may enjoy good health and that all may go well with you, even as your soul is getting along well."
3 John 1:2

Caring for your soul isn't just about the occasional bubble bath, massage, or glass of wine. While those things can offer comfort, true soul care runs deeper. It's about creating intentional rhythms—daily choices that nourish your heart, renew your mind, and strengthen your body.

Let's reflect on some simple, grace-filled ways to nurture your whole self.

Emotional Wellness

Set Boundaries with Love

Saying "no" when you need to isn't selfish—it's sacred. Healthy boundaries protect your peace and make room for what truly matters. Every time you honor your limits, you're creating space to say "yes" to what nourishes your soul.

Practice Presence

Mindfulness helps you stay grounded in the moment. Instead of rushing ahead or looking back, it allows your heart to settle into God's peace. As Philippians 4:6–7 reminds us, we're invited to bring every worry to Him in prayer—and receive peace that guards both heart and mind.

Connect with Uplifting People

You were created for connection. Spend time with those who lift your spirit, speak truth, and help you grow. As Ecclesiastes 4:9–10 says, "If either falls, one can help the other up." We're stronger when we walk together.

Journal: Create a Sacred Space

Journaling offers space to release your thoughts, process emotions, and meet with God on the page. Whether you're reflecting on scripture, pouring out a prayer, or simply writing through your day, your journal becomes a resting place for your soul.

PHYSICAL WELLNESS

"Your body is a temple of the Holy Spirit... therefore honor God with your body." 1 Corinthians 6:19–20

Your physical well-being is intricately connected to your emotional and spiritual health. These small acts of care are not only practical—they're sacred:

Move with Joy

Movement doesn't have to be intense to be impactful. Whether it's walking, stretching, dancing, or gentle yoga, find what feels good in your body. Moving with joy is a way of celebrating the life you've been given.

Nourish Your Body with Good Food

Your body deserves fuel that sustains and energizes. Choose colorful, wholesome foods—fruits, vegetables, whole grains—and give thanks for each nourishing bite. As 1 Corinthians 10:31 reminds us, "Whether you eat or drink, do it all for the glory of God."

Prioritize Rest

Sleep isn't a reward—it's a requirement. Create a calming bedtime rhythm and give yourself permission to rest. Rest is God's invitation to trust Him, knowing He never sleeps, even when you do.

Stay Hydrated

Water is one of the simplest gifts you can give your body. Staying hydrated boosts energy, focus, and overall well-being. Let it be a daily reminder that small, faithful habits lead to lasting health.

Remember, soul-care isn't about perfection—it's about intention. It's making space to care for the body, soul and spirit God entrusted to you.

You are God's beloved creation—and He delights in seeing you flourish.

Refill your cup, tend to your soul, and embrace the sacred rhythm of living fully and freely.

DECLARATION

I honor my mind, body, and spirit with love and intention— because I am worthy of care.

Reflection

What part of you—mind, body, or spirit—needs the most care right now?

What is one simple, life-giving choice you can make today to nurture your well-being and honor the way God created you?

You Are the Gardener of Your Mind

Day 23

"Don't be misled: No one makes a fool of God. What a person plants, he will harvest. The person who plants selfishness... ignores God! But the one who plants in response to God, letting God's Spirit do the growth work in him, harvests a crop of real life, eternal life."
Galatians 6:7–8 (MSG)

MINDFUL PLANTING IS essential for any garden to thrive. If you were dreaming of a flower garden filled with tulips, daffodils, and daisies, would you plant dandelions?

Of course not.

If you long for more peace, patience, or joy to blossom in your life, ask yourself: *What kind of thought seeds am I planting? What kind of thought seeds am I planting?*

Am I planting worry but hoping for peace?

Sowing frustration yet expecting patience?

Scattering judgment while craving joy and freedom?

Here's the truth: the way you think shapes how you feel—and ultimately, how you live.

Weeds will grow if you're not paying attention to the garden of your mind. And if you don't pull them out and replace them with life-giving seeds, they'll take over.

Friend, you were created for a flourishing life. If yours isn't, it might be time to notice the life-choking weeds and yank them out by the roots. Then, partner with the Master Gardener—God—to plant seeds of truth, self-compassion, gratitude, grace, and kindness.

He delights in helping you grow a beautiful, thriving life from the inside out.

DECLARATION

Little by little, I'm replacing the weeds with truth—and God is helping me grow a life I love.

Reflection

What thoughts have been growing in your mind lately—are they weeds or seeds leading to peace, joy, and truth?

What's one "weed thought" you need to pull—and what truth can you plant in its place today?

Slow Down and Let Your Soul Breathe

Day 24

"The Lord will fight for you; you need only to be still."
Exodus 14:14

YOU ARE NOT A MACHINE. Your worth isn't measured by how much you produce, how fast you move, or how much you give to others. Just like a thriving garden needs rich soil, care, and time to bloom, your soul also needs tending.

You weren't created to live in constant motion or to pour yourself out without pause. Without rest and intention, even the strongest soul begins to wear down. You don't need to try harder to be more worthy, more productive, or more valuable.

Sometimes, the most powerful act of faith is to **slow down**.

God built rest into your design. He invites you to pause, to be still, and to receive His love—not for what you do, but simply for who you are. Your soul needs grace. It needs rhythms of quiet, not constant noise.

Have you asked your soul what it needs today? Is it rest? Laughter? Silence? A moment to cry? Or maybe just time in the presence of a God who holds you gently? These are not luxuries—they're necessities.

When you slow down, breathe deeply, and let go of the need to hustle, you make space for peace to enter. You create room for healing, joy, and clarity to take root.

Think of Jesus—the One who holds all things together. He never rushed. He walked with peace, paused for people, listened deeply, and loved intentionally. He said "no" sometimes so He could say "yes" to what mattered most.

That rhythm of grace is your invitation, too. Like a rose needs sunlight to bloom, your soul needs time with the Son. You can't bloom when you're burned out. You can't give what you haven't received.

So today, friend, slow down.

Take a breath.

Listen to what your heart is truly asking for.

Let yourself rest.

Let God fill you up.

You don't need to hustle to be loved.

You are already loved.

And when you receive that love—you'll begin to flourish.

DECLARATION

I am not defined by how much I do. I am deeply loved by God, and I honor that love by creating space to rest, breathe, and be renewed.

Reflection

What is one way you've been trying to earn worth through busyness?

What does your soul truly need today—rest, joy, connection, or stillness?

Live at the Pace of Grace

Day 25

"...In quietness and trust is your strength..."
Isaiah 30:15

I KNOW HOW IT FEELS—YOU wake up and your mind is already swirling with everything you need to do. You hit the ground running, checking boxes, rushing from one thing to the next. Before you know it, the day ends in exhaustion, and you wonder, *"When will I ever have time to just breathe?"*

That was me for years—living on autopilot as a busy working mom. And now, as an empty-nester running my own business, I still catch myself slipping into that same old rhythm. Somewhere along the way, I picked up the belief that if I'm not constantly moving or producing, then I'm falling behind—or worse, failing.

But here's what I've come to learn: **busyness is not the sign of a successful life. Peace is.**

And sometimes, the most productive thing you can do is to *pause*.

When I pause to breathe and turn my attention to what truly matters, everything changes. I feel grounded, my thoughts become clearer, and I begin to extend grace to myself. It's in that space—not in my productivity—that I find lasting strength.

Think about Jesus. He didn't run from place to place. He walked. He moved with intention. He noticed people. He made time for solitude, reflection, and prayer. Jesus lived the **grace pace**—a rhythm of peace, purpose, and presence.

He knew His priorities. He wasn't afraid to say "no." And He didn't let the pressure of people or expectations pull Him out of alignment.

The **grace pace** isn't about doing nothing. It's about doing what matters—without rushing. It's about slowing down enough to hear your heart, listen to your soul, and stay rooted in God's presence.

You don't need to prove your worth through hustle. You don't need to earn God's love.

You are already loved. Already worthy. Already enough.

So today, take a deep breath.

Let go of the pressure to do it all.

Choose the grace pace—the pace of peace.

And trust that when you walk with intention and grace, everything else will fall into place.

DECLARATION

Today, I choose the pace of grace. I release the pressure to hustle and embrace the peace of walking with God.

Reflection

Where in your life are you moving too fast—and what is it costing you?

What small shift can you make to slow down and realign with what matters most?

CHOOSE PEACE
DAY 26

"And the peace of God, which surpasses all understanding, will guard your hearts and your minds in Christ Jesus."
Philippians 4:7

EVERY DAY, you're faced with a choice: to be swept up in stress or to rest in the peace that lives within you. It's not always easy. Life gets overwhelming, chaotic, and unpredictable. But in the middle of it all, you still have power. You get to choose how you'll respond.

So let me gently ask:

When life feels like too much—when plans fall apart or pressure builds —how do you respond? Do you get caught up in the storm, or can you find your footing and reach for peace, even for a moment?

Pause and reflect:

What tends to trigger your stress? What thoughts keep you spinning? How can you begin replacing those patterns with gentle practices that lead to peace? What small daily habits could help you cultivate inner calm and steady resilience?

Peace isn't something that just shows up when life is perfect. It's something you nurture—like drawing from a deep well when the surface is rough. The more often you choose peace—moment by moment—the more it becomes your rhythm. Your steady place. Your way of being. Philippians 4:7 speaks to this beautifully: *"And the peace of God, which surpasses all understanding, will guard your hearts and your minds in Christ Jesus."*

Imagine that—peace so deep, so anchored in God, it protects your heart and mind. Others might not understand it, but you'll feel it guarding you, grounding you, healing you.

Some days, peace may feel out of reach. The world can feel heavy, and stress can sit like a weight on your chest. But even then—especially then—peace is still available. Waiting to be chosen. Waiting to be received.

Stress may always show up in some form. But peace is a gift you can keep returning to. It's not a one-time fix—it's a practice. A sacred rhythm. A life-giving decision.

So today, choose peace. Not because it's easy, but because your soul needs it.

Let it slow your breath. Let it soften your heart.

Let it steady you from the inside out.

DECLARATION

Today, I choose peace. I let go of stress and welcome the calm that God freely offers my soul.

Reflection

How does your body feel when you hold onto stress—and how does it shift when you lean into peace?

What's one opportunity today to let peace guide your response instead of anxiety?

Embrace the Gift of This Moment

Day 27

"So teach us to number our days, that we may gain a heart of wisdom."
Psalm 90:12

"Lost time is never found again, and so too is an unlived life."
Unknown

HAVE you ever thought about what it means to live an *unlived* life?

It's a sobering thought. Time is one of the most precious gifts you've been given—yet it's so easy to let it slip through your fingers. You get caught up in the next task, the next worry, the endless to-do list. And with each passing moment, you can feel yourself slowly unravel—losing energy, attention, joy.

It's natural to get swept up in the busyness of daily life. You plan, strive, produce—but somewhere along the way, you forget to simply *live*. But what if today could be different?

What if you chose to fully show up—not waiting for the perfect moment, not rushing into what's next, but being fully *here*, right now?

When you rush through your days, checking off boxes, you miss the beauty tucked inside the ordinary—the warmth of sunlight on your skin, a shared laugh, a quiet pause, a long breath. These simple things are what ground you, grow you, and shape your story.

Life isn't only about what you achieve. It's about how you show up—present, open, and engaged in the moments that matter most.

So today, pause. Don't just go through the motions. Don't let your days blur into a fog of busyness.

Take a breath. Notice what's around you.

Let yourself savor it. Because at the end of your life, it won't be your accomplishments that leave the deepest mark—it will be your presence, your love, and your joy. Psalm 90:12 reminds you: "So teach us to number our days, that we may gain a heart of wisdom."

True wisdom begins when you slow down, pay attention, and become fully present. Each moment is a gift. Make it count.

Stop waiting for *someday*. Embrace the beauty of *right now*.

Be here—fully, completely.

Because this moment... this breath...

is holy ground.

DECLARATION

Today, I choose to be fully present. I will not miss the beauty of this moment.

Reflection

What distractions most often pull you away from being fully present?

What would change if you lived like *this moment* truly mattered?

Speak to Yourself
with Love
Day 28

"Finally, brothers and sisters, whatever is true, whatever is noble, whatever is right, whatever is pure, whatever is lovely, whatever is admirable—if anything is excellent or praiseworthy—think about such things."
Philippians 4:8

"You get to decide what you say to yourself."
Sadie Robertson

WHEN WAS the last time you truly paused to listen to your inner dialogue? If you haven't done that lately, now is a good time—because the way you speak to yourself shapes your peace, your day, and your life.

It's easy to blame stress or frustration on the people around you or the circumstances you can't control. But here's the truth: how you experience the world is deeply connected to what you're telling yourself about it.

It's not just about what happens—it's about how you interpret and respond to it. That's where your real power lies.

So when life feels heavy or things don't go as planned, ask yourself:

What am I saying to myself right now?

Am I offering grace—or criticism?

Would I speak these words to someone I love?

If not, know that you are deserving of the same compassion and kindness you would show to your best friend.

The way you speak to your soul matters. It impacts your emotional and spiritual well-being. It can either lift you up or weigh you down.

The truth is, **the quality of your thoughts shapes the quality of your life**. If your inner dialogue is filled with self-criticism, fear, or doubt, it's no wonder peace feels far away. But when your thoughts are kind, loving, and rooted in truth, everything starts to shift.

So today, be intentional.

Pay attention to your self-talk.

If your words are unkind, it's time to rewrite the script.

Speak words that heal, encourage, and empower you.

And when you do, your whole day will shift in a better direction.

You are worthy of a peaceful, joy-filled mind.

Let your thoughts reflect that truth.

DECLARATION

Today, I choose to speak to myself with kindness, grace, and compassion. My words will reflect the love God has for me.

Reflection

What are some common thoughts you repeat to yourself that may be hurting more than helping?

What's one kind and encouraging truth you can say to yourself today?

LET GO OF PERFECT
DAY 29

"But he said to me, 'My grace is sufficient for you, for my power is made perfect in weakness.' Therefore I will boast all the more gladly about my weaknesses, so that Christ's power may rest on me."
2 Corinthians 12:9

"God doesn't call the qualified; He qualifies the called."
Unknown

IT's time to let go of the lie that you need to be perfect. You're not perfect—and you don't have to be. Deep down, you already know that, but the pressure to *do more*, *be more*, and *never falter* still finds a way to creep in.

You hold yourself to impossible standards. You try to do it all, be everything to everyone, and never drop the ball. But that grind for perfection? It quietly drains your peace, your joy, and your freedom.

Think about it: How often does your inner critic whisper, *"You should've done better... You didn't do enough... Someone else could've handled this better*"? You're not alone. Those thoughts can echo like a broken record. But here's the truth: **Perfection is a myth.**

When you chase it, you miss what matters most—peace, connection, joy, and the deep assurance that who you are is already enough. You weren't created to live under that pressure. You were created for **grace**. Grace from God. Grace for yourself. Grace that lifts the burden and reminds you—you don't have to measure up to anyone else's impossible expectations.

Picture this: Jesus gently cups your face, looks into your eyes, and says, *"Breathe. Let it go. I'm not asking you to be perfect. I already love you as you are."* What a relief, right? The only Perfect One doesn't expect perfection from you. He simply wants your heart. You don't have to prove anything. You don't have to earn His love.

It's already yours—completely and unconditionally. Jesus didn't go to the cross so you could keep striving. He did it so you could live freely, knowing His grace is enough. It's not about perfection—it's about transformation.

You grow and become more like Him—not to earn His love, but *because* you are already deeply loved. So today, release the weight of perfection. Let grace be your rhythm. Let it guide you, comfort you, and remind you: you are enough, simply because you're His.

DECLARATION

I let go of perfection and choose grace. I am fully loved, fully accepted, and enough just as I am.

Reflection

How would it feel to release the need to be perfect and embrace being fully loved by God?

What unrealistic expectations have you been placing on yourself lately?

You Get to Choose How to Respond

Day 30

"If it is possible, as far as it depends on you, live at peace with everyone."
Romans 12:18

"You may not control all the events that happen to you, but you can decide not to be reduced by them."
Maya Angelou

Do you ever feel like the weight of others' words or actions drags you down—especially when those closest to you unintentionally trigger your emotions? Does your mood shift with the chaos around you or the headlines that flash across your screen?

It can be overwhelming, can't it? The world has a way of pushing and pulling on one's heart, but here's a truth worth remembering: **you get to choose how you respond.**

Even when life feels chaotic, you have the power to anchor yourself in peace. You are not at the mercy of every conversation, comment, or crisis. You can decide what kind of energy you bring into each moment.

If you're like me, you've had moments when your reactions took over—when something triggered you and you were swept up in a wave of frustration or hurt. But what if, instead of reacting, you paused, took a breath, and chose peace instead of chaos?

I'm not saying it's easy—it isn't. But it's possible. And it's powerful. When you feel pressure building or negativity creeping in, choose to **observe, not absorb.** Breathe deeply. Release the need to take everything personally. Just because things feel out of control doesn't mean *you* have to be. That's your power.

You are the gatekeeper of your emotions. You decide how to respond. And that's where real strength lies.

When you choose peace in the midst of chaos, you create a sanctuary within yourself—one that external circumstances cannot touch. When you choose kindness, you not only protect your own heart but create a ripple of calm that can soften the hearts around you too.

So next time your emotions rise, pause and reflect. You don't have to let the outside world dictate your internal state. You can choose a better way. And God is with you in that choice.

Let your peace rise.

Be calm in the storm.

Lead with kindness—and watch what shifts in you and around you.

DECLARATION

Today, I choose to respond with peace, not chaos. I lead with kindness, because God's peace lives in me.

Reflection

What situations tend to pull you into chaos or reactivity?

What phrase or scripture could you keep close to help you pause in moments of pressure?

Gratitude with New Eyes

Day 31

"Give thanks in all circumstances; for this is God's will for you in Christ Jesus.
1 Thessalonians 5:18

WANT to feel more grateful in an instant? Try this simple, soul-shifting practice:

Instead of only listing what you're thankful for—imagine your life without it.

It's called "mental subtraction of positive events." That might sound clinical, but the heart behind it is beautifully spiritual. It invites you to pause, reflect, and truly see how precious your blessings are.

Think about something or someone you treasure—your spouse, a child, a friend, your home, your health, or your work.

Now picture how easily that blessing could've never come into your life.

What if you never crossed paths?

What if that door had stayed shut?

What if a single decision had gone a different way?

When you pause to consider what might have been, you begin to cherish what is.

This mindset shift awakens deep gratitude—not just for the good gifts themselves, but for the grace that brought them to you.

It's like seeing your life with fresh eyes.

And the ripple effects are powerful—more peace, deeper joy, greater contentment, and stronger relationships. Gratitude truly nourishes the soul.

So today, instead of chasing "more," take a moment to thank God for what already is.

The people you love.

The memories that shaped you.

The divine detours that protected you.

The unexpected gifts that still bring tears to your eyes.

These are sacred blessings—worth remembering, savoring, and holding close.

DECLARATION

Today, I thank God not only for what I have, but for the grace that allowed it to be part of my life.

Reflection

What is one gift or relationship in your life that you sometimes take for granted—but couldn't imagine life without?

How might reflecting on "what might have been" help you appreciate your present blessings even more?

LET GO OF EXPECTATIONS

DAY 32

"Be still before the Lord and wait patiently for him."
Psalm 37:7a

LET'S BE HONEST—THERE'S probably a part of you that really wants things to go *your* way. You're not alone. That's only human.

You carry expectations every day:

That the car will start.

That the lights will turn on.

That people will be kind and thoughtful.

That your children will behave.

That your efforts will be noticed and appreciated.

That you'll have the strength to get through.

That God will answer your prayers the way you hope.

There's comfort in believing life will go according to plan. But the truth? It often doesn't. People disappoint. Plans shift. And sometimes, the answers you pray for don't come in the form you expect. When that happens, you have a choice:

Will you let unmet expectations steal your peace? Will you resist what's happening—or will you release and trust? The more you resist what *is*, the more you add to your own suffering. But when you choose to let go —to release your grip on control and surrender the outcome—you make space for peace. Because peace doesn't come from perfect circumstances. It comes from surrender.

So the next time life throws a curveball, pause. Breathe. Acknowledge your feelings, but don't let them run the show. You don't have to be perfect. Life doesn't either. You were never meant to carry it all. You were created to trust the One who's already carrying you.

Letting go doesn't mean giving up. It means opening up. Opening to grace. To trust. To peace. God is with you in every twist and turn. He is faithful in every unfolding moment.

So let go of the pressure to hold it all together. Trust the process. Live in the moment. You're exactly where you need to be.

And so is God.

DECLARATION

I release the need to control and trust God with what I cannot see. I choose peace over pressure and faith over fear.

Reflection

How do you feel when things don't go as planned—and what do you usually tell yourself in those moments?

Where would you like to invite God's peace in place of your pressure?

Smiling is Soul Care

Day 33

"A happy heart makes the face cheerful, but heartache crushes the spirit."
Proverbs 15:13

THERE's something about a smile that holds the power to shift the energy of your day—and the world around you. It's such a simple gesture, yet its effect can be profound.

As I write this, I can't help but smile myself—because even now, it feels like an act of soul care. I want to remind you today: **you hold that power too.** How often do you truly smile—not just out of habit, but as an intentional act of joy?

A smile can be like a breath of fresh air—restoring, calming, energizing. When you smile, you invite goodness into your own heart and share it with others. It costs nothing, yet it gives so much.

I was reminded of this recently when my husband turned to me and asked, "What are you smiling about?" The funny thing was—I hadn't even realized I *was* smiling. I was simply sitting in peace, lost in thought. But somehow my face had softened, and joy had quietly made its way in.

Just like that, my smile became his smile. A small, unspoken exchange—but it lifted both of our spirits.

That's when I realized: a smile is nourishment. It's self-care in its gentlest form. It invites your heart to soften, even when life feels heavy. Here are just a few reasons why smiling is worth the effort:

It can make you look younger and more vibrant.

It lifts your mood and releases feel-good chemicals.

It's been proven to bring more pleasure to the brain than chocolate!

Even a *forced* smile can improve your mood.

It makes you appear more kind, approachable, and confident.

And—it's contagious. Your smile spreads light beyond you.

So, if you're feeling stressed or weighed down, just try smiling. Even if it begins as a choice, not a feeling, it creates a shift. Smiling helps you reconnect, reframe, and gently push back against heaviness. It's not about pretending things are perfect. It's about *welcoming joy back in—* even if only for a moment.

Wear your smile like a badge of strength and quiet beauty. Let it be a reflection of the love and light already in you. You never know how your smile might brighten someone else's day—even your own.

DECLARATION

Today, I choose to smile—with intention, with kindness, and with joy. My smile is a reflection of God's love in me.

Reflection

How does your body and mind feel after you smile—even if you didn't feel like it at first?

What's something you can do today that might bring a smile to someone else's face?

Be a Friend to Yourself

Day 34

"The tongue has the power of life and death, and those who love it will eat its fruit."
Proverbs 18:21

How often do you show more grace and compassion to others than you do to yourself? You cheer on your friends with patience, understanding, and love. Yet when it comes to your own mistakes, your inner voice can be your harshest critic. It's easy to fall into the trap of negative self-talk—and it's one of the most soul-draining habits we carry.

Let me ask you a few questions:

Take a moment to reflect and rate yourself on the following statements using a scale of **1 to 10 (1 = Not true at all, 10 = Completely true)**:

I have spoken to myself with kindness, hope, and love this week.
I have been patient with myself when things don't go as planned.
I celebrated my wins, no matter how small.
I extended grace to myself when I stumbled or fell short.
I believe in the potential God has placed inside me.

My inner dialogue this week has been more self-affirming than self-critical.

Too many people say, *"I'm my own worst enemy,"* and it breaks my heart —because that kind of thinking is rooted in lies. Lies that come from unrealistic expectations, past wounds, or voices that never should have had power. But here's the truth: **self-doubt and self-loathing are tools of the enemy to keep you stuck and steal your joy.**

You were handcrafted by God.

You are fearfully and wonderfully made.

You are His masterpiece.

How you speak to yourself matters. Your words shape your heart, your choices, and your future. That's why today, I want to challenge you: **be a friend to yourself.** Speak with the same tenderness, love, and encouragement you offer others. Be gentle with your mistakes. Celebrate your growth. Don't let the voice of shame drown out the voice of truth. The enemy wants you to feel small—but God calls you *beloved.* The kinder you are to yourself, the lighter your spirit becomes. The more grace you show inwardly, the more peace you carry outwardly.

So today, pause and listen to your inner voice. And if it isn't kind, speak back with love and truth. You are worthy of your own compassion.

DECLARATION

Today, I choose to treat myself like a friend and remember I am loved by God.

Reflection

How would your life change if you spoke to yourself like someone you love?

What kind, encouraging words do you need to hear from yourself today?

Embrace the Gift
of Rest

Day 35

*"Then Jesus said, 'Come to me, all of you who are weary and carry
heavy burdens, and I will give you rest.'"*
Matthew 11:28 (NLT)

THERE IS SO much joy waiting for you in the simple act of slowing
down. In a world that constantly demands more—more effort, more
productivity, more noise—it can feel almost impossible to take a step
back. But what if slowing down is exactly what your soul is craving?

God, in His wisdom, set aside one day out of every seven as a day of rest
—Sabbath. This isn't just a nice idea; it's a sacred invitation. It's a
rhythm of restoration that reconnects you with your spirit—the part of
you that is free from stress, striving, and overwhelm.

When you skip that rest, when you keep running at full speed, something starts to suffer. You feel scattered, weary, and emotionally
depleted. That constant motion takes a toll—not just on your body, but
on your heart, your mind, and your connection with God.

Sabbath isn't just about sleeping in or catching up on chores—though
rest can certainly include those things. It's about stopping. Breathing.

Remembering who you are and who God is. It's about shifting from doing to being, and letting God meet you right where you are.

He created this rhythm of rest because He knows how easily you fall into the trap of hustle and distraction. And when you're always in motion, you miss the beauty of the present moment—the small gifts, the ordinary miracles, and the still, small voice of your Creator.

Slowing down isn't only about taking a day off. It's about being more present in every moment. It's pausing before you react. Creating room to think, feel, and be. When you allow yourself to slow down, you make space for clarity, gratitude, and deeper connection. You begin to see what really matters—and how you want to show up in the world.

Here's the truth: with every word and action, you're shaping your legacy. What others remember most won't be how much you accomplished, but how you made them feel. Were you hurried and distracted —or present and grounded?

So take that deep breath. Let go of the pressure. Notice the goodness that's still here, even in the mess. Give yourself grace. And above all, remember this: you are deeply loved.

This is your invitation—slow down, create space for peace, and embrace the quiet gift of Sabbath. Let it restore you. Not just for today, but for the journey ahead.

DECLARATION

I give myself permission to slow down. In rest, I reconnect with God, with myself, and with what truly matters.

Reflection

What areas of your life feel rushed or constantly busy?

How do you feel physically and emotionally when you go too long without rest?

Speak with Intention and Grace

Day 36

"A gentle answer turns away wrath, but a harsh word stirs up anger."
Proverbs 15:1

WE ALL HAVE THOSE MOMENTS. You know the ones: when emotions rise, tempers flare, and every word feels like a spark ready to ignite. Maybe it's an argument with a loved one, a misunderstanding with a friend, or a frustration with someone you care about. It's so easy in those moments to just let it all spill out, to lash out with words that come from anger or frustration. But what if you paused? What if, instead of reacting in the heat of the moment, you chose to slow down and breathe?

In my own life, I've learned the hard way that those knee-jerk reactions —the ones where I let my feelings take over—rarely end well. They often lead to hurt, regret, and distance. But when I choose to slow down, take a breath, and really think before I speak, it changes everything. *It's in slowing down that we give ourselves the space to choose words that heal, rather than wound.*

When you're in the middle of a disagreement and your heart starts racing, take a step back. Breathe deeply. Remind yourself of the love you have for this person and that their feelings matter just as much as yours. This isn't about winning. It's about understanding. It's about honoring the relationship above being "right." Because when you speak out of anger, you're not communicating—you're reacting. And reacting rarely builds bridges.

Proverbs 15:1 tells us, *"A gentle answer turns away wrath, but a harsh word stirs up anger."* I've seen this truth play out in my own life. In those heated moments, the power of a gentle word can diffuse the tension and bring calm. But the sharpness of a harsh word? It only fans the flames. When you slow down to speak with intention, you create an opening for healing, for connection, for understanding.

This isn't easy, I know. It takes practice and patience, especially when emotions are running high. But if we want relationships that are rooted in trust and love, then we have to be intentional with our words. So, the next time you feel your heart racing and your words rushing to the surface, take a pause. Count to ten. Breathe. And then speak with kindness, with intention, with love.

Remember this: Your words have incredible power. They can heal, or they can hurt. They can build, or they can destroy. So, choose wisely. Speak the truth but always in love. *"Be slow to speak, and quick to listen."* (James 1:19) Because in those pauses, you make space for what matters most—connection.

DECLARATION

I choose to pause, breathe, and speak with love. My words are guided by grace, not emotion.

Reflection

When was the last time you reacted before pausing—and what was the outcome?

How might your relationships shift if you slowed down and listened more?

PATIENCE IS SOUL CARE
DAY 37

*"But if we hope for what we do not see, we wait for it with
patience."*
Romans 8:25 (ESV)

WE'VE all heard the saying "patience is a virtue" more times than we
can count—but let's be honest: when it's *your* turn to practice it, it's a
whole different story. You know it's something you *should* have, but
wow—it can be tough, especially when you're waiting for something
you deeply want or need. But here's the truth: developing patience is
one of the most powerful things you can do, because it shapes you into
someone who can wait with grace, peace, and even joy.

You're not alone in your impatience. We've all been there—waiting for a
breakthrough, a relationship to shift, healing to come, or a long-held
dream to finally take shape. Maybe you're in that space right now.
Maybe you've had those nights where the clock seems frozen and your
hope feels stretched thin. But don't miss this: waiting doesn't mean
nothing is happening.

Patience is a faith muscle. It's choosing to believe that God is still
moving behind the scenes, even when you can't see it. It's releasing your

grip on control and trusting that His timing is wiser, kinder, and far better than anything you could rush.

Even in the seasons where it feels like you're standing still—you are growing. You are becoming. God's Word reminds you that patience is a fruit of the Spirit (Galatians 5:22), which means it's not something you have to manufacture on your own. It's something that flows from staying close to Jesus. The more you abide in Him—like a branch staying connected to the vine—the more patience begins to grow naturally in you.

Think about how patient Jesus has been with you. With your doubts. Your missteps. Your wandering. His patience hasn't wavered, and as you walk with Him, He'll teach you to extend that same patience to yourself, to others, and to your circumstances.

Here's the challenge: sometimes you get so focused on what you're waiting for, that you miss what God is doing *in* the waiting. But it's in those quiet, in-between spaces where God often does His most meaningful work. He's refining you. Strengthening you. Preparing you for what's ahead. If you got what you wanted the moment you wanted it, you might miss some of the deepest lessons in trust, resilience, and gratitude.

Looking back, you'll probably see that some of your most transformative growth happened in the waiting—not just in the arrival. So if you're feeling impatient today, pause. Breathe. Remind yourself that slow progress doesn't mean *no* progress. In fact, sometimes what looks like delay is actually God's grace giving you the time your heart needs to fully receive what's coming. He's not late. He's present. And He's working. Lean into His love. Let His patience carry you. The best is still unfolding—one faithful step at a time.

DECLARATION

I trust God in the waiting. I may not see it yet, but I believe He is working in me, preparing me, and growing me every step of the way.

Reflection

What are you currently waiting on that's testing your patience?

How can you lean more deeply into God's timing instead of your own?

Have Fun and Play!
Day 38

"A cheerful heart is good medicine, but a crushed spirit dries up the bones."
Proverbs 17:22

WHEN WAS the last time you truly played? I mean the kind of play where you completely forget about responsibilities, dive into spontaneity, embrace creativity, and laugh so hard your stomach hurts. When was the last time you got so lost in an activity that time just slipped away, and you couldn't help but smile at the joy of it all?

I'll be the first to confess: this is an area where I could definitely do better. Every day, my to-do list grows longer, and being "productive" takes priority over the playful side of me. It's way easier to focus on what I **have** to do than to make room for what I **want** to do. And yet, when I finally give myself permission to play—when I let go of the pressure and tap into my carefree spirit—it feels like a fresh breeze on a warm summer day. It's energizing, light, and exactly what my soul needs.

So, what's the cost when we forget how to play? It's easy to lose our spark, to watch our creativity wither, and to get buried under stress. Life becomes about surviving the grind rather than thriving in the fullness of joy that God designed for us. We start to forget that play is more than having fun—it's a vital part of our well-being.

Your soul needs to play. You need laughter, silly moments, and the freedom to explore life without rules or expectations. Play brings you back to life. It lightens your heart and reminds you that life isn't always about checking boxes or handling "serious business." It's about feeling alive—about remembering what it means to have fun.

What are you pushing aside in the name of your endless to-do list? What passions, silly joys, or simple pleasures have quietly slipped away?

Maybe today's the day to press pause, set the heavy stuff aside, and let yourself reconnect with that playful, curious, free part of you. You were made for joy that makes you laugh out loud, and creativity that stirs something deep within you. The world needs your light, your laughter, and that beautiful spark of playfulness inside you.

Go ahead—take that dance break in the kitchen, pick up the paintbrush, or finally try that hobby you've been daydreaming about. It's in those carefree, joy-filled moments that you reconnect with who you really are.

You shine brightest when you're not just pushing through life, but actually enjoying it. Play isn't a luxury. It's essential soul care. So give yourself permission to have fun. Laugh loudly. Let your spirit breathe.You were made for this kind of joy.

DECLARATION

I give myself permission to play, laugh, and enjoy life. Joy is not a distraction—it's sacred nourishment for my soul.

Reflection

When was the last time you played just for the joy of it?

What would it look like to make space for play this week?

Tend Your Soul One Page at a Time

Day 39

"Trust in him at all times, you people; pour out your hearts to him, for God is our refuge."
Psalm 62:8

Have you been burning the candle at both ends—hustling to meet demands, crossing off to-do lists, and serving everyone around you?

Do you collapse into bed at night, completely spent?

Are you constantly prioritizing others while quietly neglecting yourself?

Let's be honest—many of us are high-capacity, big-hearted people who pour ourselves out day after day. But here's the truth: your well-being is your responsibility. And if you don't make it a priority now, eventually your body, mind, or spirit will demand that you do.

Want to know one simple, often overlooked way to care for yourself? Journaling. Here are three gentle but powerful ways journaling helps foster an abundant mindset and a healthy soul:

Journaling Helps You Take Ownership of Your Well-Being

Each day, pause and ask: Are the choices I'm making leading me toward joy and health?

Journaling creates sacred space to slow down, check in, and honor what you really need. It gives you permission to name your feelings, acknowledge your overwhelm, and recognize what's been neglected.

This isn't selfish—it's *responsible.*

When you tend to yourself, you show up with calm, clarity, and compassion—not just for others, but for you.

Journaling Helps You Process Emotions Honestly

Do you bottle things up or silence your emotions to avoid rocking the boat? Maybe you've told yourself that being strong means ignoring how you feel. But strength without honesty becomes burnout.

Journaling invites you to speak the truth to yourself.

It gives you a safe space to say the hard things and remember—loving yourself isn't prideful. It's essential.

Journaling Builds an Abundant Mindset

When life feels like a blur of routines and responsibilities, it's easy to miss the beauty in front of you. Journaling slows you down long enough to notice it. Gratitude, reflection, and presence—these are muscles you build when you write. And over time, you begin to see more clearly the joy, goodness, and growth that are already part of your story. It also gives you the chance to challenge old thought patterns and replace them with truth.

So today, grab your journal (or write in the space provided here.) Start with one sentence. One feeling. One prayer. You don't need perfect words—just a willing heart. Let journaling become a sacred practice for tending your inner life.

DECLARATION

Writing from the heart is how I meet God and care for my soul.

What emotions have you been avoiding that journaling could help you process?

What's one small joy you can write down and be grateful for today?

Tend Your Own Grass

Day 40

"Pay careful attention to your own work, for then you will get the satisfaction of a job well done, and you won't need to compare yourself to anyone else. For we are each responsible for our own conduct."
Galatians 6:4–5 (NLT)

Social media loves to whisper the lie: *The grass is always greener on the other side.*

It's easy to believe that what someone else has must be better than what you've got. Their life looks shinier. Their house more peaceful. Their marriage more romantic. Their career more successful.

But here's the truth: you're usually seeing someone else's highlight reel while living in your own behind-the-scenes footage.

So pause. Shift your focus.

Instead of wishing for someone else's life, how about nurturing your own?

Tend to the grass beneath your feet.

Water the relationships you already have.

Pay attention to the dreams God has already planted in your heart.

Show up for your life with presence and purpose.

I was reminded of this truth while holding my one-month-old grandson. As I snuggled in close—breathing in his newborn scent, listening to his tiny squeaks—I was overwhelmed by the sacredness of that ordinary moment.

He didn't have to do anything to be loved. He simply is. And so are you.

Somewhere along the way, you may have absorbed the lie that your value comes from accomplishments, accolades, or people-pleasing. But from the moment you were born, you were already worthy of love.

You don't have to prove yourself.

You just need to be who God created you to be.

You are not behind.

You are not lacking.

You are not less than.

You are exactly where you're meant to be—right here.

Focus your energy on watering the beautiful grass you're standing on.

DECLARATION

Today, I choose to nurture the life I've been given. I release comparison and receive God's love for me, just as I am.

In what area of your life have you been tempted to compare or feel "behind"?

What would it look like to water the grass you're standing on today?

PART FOUR
PESTS AND WEEDS—
OVERCOME SPIRITUAL
HINDRANCES

Every garden faces threats—pests that devour and weeds that choke out growth. In the same way, fear, doubt, sin, and distraction can quietly creep in, threatening the beauty and purpose God has planted in your life.

In this section, you'll be invited to recognize and gently remove the spiritual hindrances that hold you back. These daily readings will help you identify what's crowding your soul and make room for God's truth to take deeper root.

With His strength, you *can* overcome anything that tries to steal your joy, block your peace, or silence your purpose.

Take a breath. Lean in. Let's clear the soil of your soul—and watch what God will grow.

Healing Begins With Honesty

Day 41

The Lord is near to the brokenhearted and saves the crushed in spirit."
Psalm 34:18

BEFORE WE BEGIN this next part of the journey, take a deep breath. You've already begun something sacred—choosing to tend to the garden of your soul with intention and care. If you're still here, dear friend, it's not by accident. You've made space in your life to show up, to seek peace, and to invite God into deeper places. That is holy work.

The past 40 days have been about planting seeds of truth, remembering your identity in Christ, and nourishing your soul. But now comes the deeper digging—the part where we gently begin to uproot what's been quietly growing beneath the surface. Every flourishing garden has its weeds. Fear. Shame. Anger. Regret. Self-doubt. They take root quietly. They grow quickly. But by God's grace—they can be pulled out.

This section is about emotional healing. It may feel tender. Uncomfortable. Like untangling the hidden roots that have been wrapped around your heart for far too long. But don't be discouraged. Healing begins with honesty—not fixing, not hiding, but simply honoring what you feel.

It begins here—with permission. Permission to feel what you feel. Permission to tell the truth. Permission to welcome grace in, even where the pain still lingers. You might begin by naming what's there:

"I'm feeling ___, and it's okay to feel this way."

Then speak gently to your own soul, like you would to someone you love:

"Sweetheart, I know this is hard. You're allowed to feel this. I'm here with you. God is here with you. We'll get through this together."

These words won't erase the pain, but they soften it. They create space for God's healing love to take root. And don't underestimate the power of raw, honest prayer. You don't need polished words—just truth. Let your tears speak if they need to. Let your silence speak. God is near to the brokenhearted, not afraid of your pain but present in it.

The Psalms remind us again and again: God draws close to those who pour out their hearts. The messy, tangled, aching places are often the very soil where His deepest healing begins. You don't have to heal overnight. But today, you can take one step closer to wholeness—by honoring what's real and letting God meet you there.

DECLARATION

I honor my emotions and invite God into every part of my heart. I am healing, growing, and deeply loved.

Reflection

When was the last time you allowed yourself to feel something without judgment or rushing to fix it?

What is one honest prayer your soul needs today—even if it's only a whispered sentence?

THE TRUTH ABOUT
WHO YOU REALLY ARE

DAY 42

"For we are God's masterpiece. He has created us anew in Christ Jesus, so we can do the good things he planned for us long ago."
Ephesians 2:10 (NLT)

YOU WERE CREATED FOR A DEEP, eternal love relationship with God. He has a beautiful plan for your life. But just as God calls you into His love, the enemy works tirelessly to distort and destroy your understanding of who you are in Christ.

Satan is a master of deception, and one of his most powerful tactics is attacking your identity. He whispers lies, hoping you'll believe them and forget the truth of who you are. But today, let's expose those lies—and replace them with the truth of God's Word:

> **LIE:** *You are worthless and unlovable.*
> **TRUTH:** *You are fearfully and wonderfully made by a God who loves you beyond measure. Your worth is defined by the One who created you.*
> **LIE:** *You are defined by your past.*
> **TRUTH:** *In Christ, you are a new creation. When you turn to*

Jesus, He forgives you completely. Your identity is rooted in His grace, not your history.
LIE: *You are not good enough.*
TRUTH: *God has uniquely designed you with gifts, talents, and purpose. You are chosen, called, and equipped by Him.*
LIE: *You are alone and abandoned.*
TRUTH: *God promises to be with you always. You are never alone. You belong to Him and are part of His family.*

When those lies creep in—and they will—don't just listen to them. Fight back with truth. Your identity doesn't come from your mistakes, your achievements, or what others say about you. It comes from who God says you are.

"See what great love the Father has lavished on us, that we should be called children of God! And that is what we are!" 1 John 3:1 You are God's child. You carry His image and reflect a piece of His heart that no one else can. Your life is meant to shine with His glory. And the more you trust Him and walk in His truth, the more His light shines through you.

So, if you've ever felt lost, unworthy, or unsure of where you belong—remember this: You are loved. You are chosen. Abundant life is your birthright in Christ.

DECLARATION

I am God's masterpiece—fully loved, deeply chosen, and created with purpose. My identity is rooted in His truth, not the lies of the enemy.

Reflection

When you think about your identity, whose voice are you listening to—
God's truth or the enemy's lies?

What's one truth from God's Word you want to start speaking over
yourself each day?

God's Love Isn't
Complicated
Day 43

"But God demonstrates His own love for us in this: While we were
still sinners, Christ died for us."
Romans 5:8

IF YOU'RE anything like me, you've probably made your relationship
with God more complicated than it needs to be. You might catch yourself setting impossibly high expectations for how you "should" be living
out your faith:

You should wake up early for an hour-long quiet time.

You should serve every week at church.

You should bring up Jesus in every conversation.

You should always be strong, always be growing, always be "doing."

And if you don't? You start believing the lie: *I must not be doing enough.*
I must not be enough. It's like a weed that was most likely planted in
childhood or early adulthood—maybe from people-pleasing, perfectionism, or performance-driven environments.

For me, I remember striving to impress my teachers—believing that if I performed well, I'd be accepted and loved. And without realizing it, I carried that same weed into my walk with God.

If I act right, He'll love me.

If I do all the right things, I'll be worthy.

If I check the boxes, then I'm acceptable.

Maybe you've carried those weeds too. The problem is, those thoughts take up space where truth is meant to grow. They crowd out peace and joy, replacing them with striving, guilt, and exhaustion. But here's the truth that changed everything for me:

God never planted those expectations—we did. And now it's time to pull them up.

The idea that you have to earn God's love is one of the most persistent weeds in the soul garden—and one of the most damaging. Because God's love isn't earned. It's already yours.

Your worth isn't based on performance.

It's not found in your spiritual checklist.

It's not in how many Bible studies you've completed or how perfectly you've behaved.

Your worth is rooted in who you are—God's creation. His beloved.

John 3:16 doesn't say, "for God so loved the world when they got it all right."

It says, *"For God so loved the world that He gave..."*

He loved. So He gave.

No conditions. No striving. No proof required.

When you remember that God's love is a gift—not a reward—it changes everything. Walking with Him stops being a performance and becomes a relationship.

Not forced devotion. Not duty-driven checklists. But simple connection —honest, open, loving.

Think about the people you love most. You don't want them to spend time with you out of guilt. You want to be with them because of love. And God feels the same about you.

So pull up the weeds of perfectionism.

Tear out the "shoulds" that have taken over your faith.

Clear the space for something better—grace, rest, and joy.

Now, imagine Jesus sitting on your couch—not impatient, not keeping score, just present. Or picture Him at the back door, waiting to walk with you. Not demanding. Not disappointed. Just near. Just loving you.

You don't have to prove a thing.

You already belong.

So stop striving.

Start receiving.

And walk with the One who already calls you His.

DECLARATION

I am loved by God, not because of what I do, but because of who I am—His. I release striving and rest in His grace.

Where have you been trying to earn God's love or approval?

How does it feel to imagine God loving you exactly as you are, right now?

FEEL WHAT HURTS
DAY 44

"So do not fear, for I am with you; do not be dismayed, for I am your God. I will strengthen you and help you; I will uphold you with my righteous right hand."
Isaiah 41:10

WHEN WE'RE in deep pain, our first instinct is often to run.

We distract ourselves. We push the grief down. We bury it beneath busyness, entertainment, or sheer willpower—anything to avoid feeling the weight of sorrow.

And sometimes, in the short term, that's okay.

There are moments when we have to carry on—when life demands decisions, when loved ones need us, or when we simply need to get through the day.

But as a long-term strategy?

Avoiding pain only delays healing.

It's like trying to hold a beach ball underwater. You can keep it down for a while, but eventually the pressure builds—and it bursts to the surface.

Our emotions work the same way. If we don't tend to them, they'll find other ways to get our attention—often in ways we never intended.

Grief doesn't only follow the death of a loved one.

It shows up in many forms—loss of a relationship, a dream, your health, your sense of safety, or a version of life you imagined.

And in order to heal, grief must be named.

There are seasons when the most courageous thing you can do is simply sit with your sorrow. To feel what hurts. To acknowledge what's been lost. To offer compassion to your own weary heart.

I've walked through this myself—especially after losing both of my parents.

Sometimes, the grief would rise out of nowhere—a song, a scent, a photo, a memory.

At first, those moments overwhelmed me.

But when I stopped running and started listening to my heart, something changed.

The grief didn't disappear, but it softened.

Memories began to hold warmth as well as ache. Gratitude joined the sadness.

And eventually, laughter came too.

Healing never happens in a straight line.

But with time, patience, and God's presence, it does happen.

So take a breath.

Call on Jesus.

Feel what you feel.

Be patient with yourself—because you are worth that care.

And one day, you'll feel the sunlight again.

Joy will return.

And your garden—the one grief threatened—will bloom in a whole new way.

DECLARATION

*I don't have to rush my healing. **God meets me in my grief with gentleness, love, and strength.***

Reflection

What part of my pain have I been avoiding or pushing down?

What would it look like to sit with that pain instead of running from it?

SET DOWN YOUR
SHAME

DAY 45

"Therefore, there is now no condemnation for those who are in
Christ Jesus."
Romans 8:1

YOU'VE BEEN THERE. You've said or done things you wish you could take back. The words replay in your mind. The moment loops on repeat.

You think, *If only I had... If only I hadn't...* And then guilt settles in—heavy, suffocating, relentless. But guilt rarely stays quiet. It often twists into shame, whispering that your mistakes define you. That you're too much—or not enough. That maybe, just maybe, you've gone too far for grace.

But friend, hear this:

You are not beyond grace. Yes, you've made mistakes—we all have. Some small, some life-altering. If your actions have caused harm to yourself or others, there may be consequences. But you do not have to carry guilt forever. That weight was never meant to be yours. So how do you let go?

Own your mistake. Be honest about where things went wrong—not to shame yourself, but to grow. Try saying, *"I messed up when I___. I'm truly sorry. I can't change the past, but with God's help, I can do better."*

Stop punishing yourself.

Reliving the pain, refusing to forgive yourself, allowing shame to keep you stuck—none of that changes what happened. It only steals your peace.

Receive grace.

God isn't standing over you in judgment. He's kneeling beside you in compassion. He lifts your chin and gently says, *"Let Me help you move forward."* God already knows your imperfections. He knows where you've fallen short. And still—His love has not changed. His mercy has not wavered. His grace has not run out.

If guilt has made you want to hide from God, please remember this:

God isn't waiting to punish you... He's drawing near. He's saying, *"Come to Me. Let Me lift this burden. Let Me restore your soul."*

There is nothing—*nothing*—you could ever do that would make Him stop loving you. Not even your biggest mistake. Jesus already went to the cross for that. Your failures don't disqualify you from grace. They're the very reason grace was given.

So today, let it go. Lay down the guilt. Set aside the shame. And take hold of the truth:

You are still His.

Still seen.

Still loved.

Still welcome.

God doesn't love you because of what you've done—or haven't done.

You can't earn it. You can't lose it.

He loves you simply because you are:

His creation.

His child.

His beloved.

That's the truth.

You can resist it.

You can believe the lie that you have to prove yourself.

Or...you can rest in the freedom of knowing Jesus already did the work.

So today—please receive it.

Let it soak in.

Let it change how you walk through your day.

Lay it all down.

Step into the freedom of knowing—you are deeply loved, fully forgiven, and gently held.

DECLARATION

I release the weight of guilt and receive God's grace. I am forgiven, free, and fully loved.

Reflection

What guilt or regret have you been silently carrying?

Have you truly received God's grace in that area—or are you still trying to earn His love?

You Are Lovable No Matter What

Day 46

"Though my father and mother forsake me, the Lord will receive me."

Psalm 27:10

LIFE IS TOO SHORT—AND too precious—to believe you're unlovable just because someone else didn't know how to love you.

Rejection and abandonment are among the deepest wounds the soul can carry. Whether it came from a parent, a spouse, a friend, or someone you trusted with your heart, the sting of being overlooked, dismissed, or left behind can leave lasting scars. And often, that pain whispers a cruel lie: *You're not worth loving.* But hear me, friend—that is not the voice of truth.

That is a lie straight from the pit of hell. If you've ever believed it, even for a moment, let this sink in:

You are lovable.

You always have been.

You always will be.

Someone else's inability to love you well says more about their limitations than your worth. Their rejection is not a reflection of your value. Their absence does not diminish your presence in God's heart. You were formed in love by the One who knows you fully and calls you *beloved*.

Your Creator doesn't just tolerate you—He delights in you. He receives you. He embraces you. He stays. His love isn't fragile. It doesn't depend on your performance or your past.

It doesn't falter when others walk away.

It's steady. Unshakable. Forever.

So today, release the belief that someone else's failure to love you means you're unworthy of love. Let go of the pain that told you you weren't enough.

You are already enough in God's eyes.

You are chosen, cherished, and completely received.

You may have been rejected by people, but you have never been rejected by God.

You are held.

You are safe.

You are deeply, eternally loved.

DECLARATION

I am deeply loved, fully accepted, and forever held by God—even when others have walked away.

Reflection

Whose rejection have you been carrying that still shapes how you see yourself?

How would your life change if you truly believed—every day—that you are loved and accepted just as you are by God?

BREAK FREE FROM SELF-PITY

DAY 47

"And we know that in all things God works for the good of those who love Him, who have been called according to His purpose."
Romans 8:28

AT SOME POINT, life knocks you down. Hard.

Maybe it already has.

Disappointment, betrayal, rejection, sickness, failure—whatever the struggle, it's easy to slip into the pit of self-pity. When things fall apart, when people hurt you, when your body breaks down or the weight of life feels unbearable, self-pity can feel like a safe place to land.

And if you're honest, sometimes it even feels justified. But here's the problem: self-pity doesn't just visit—it takes root. And if you don't tend to it, it becomes a weed that quietly chokes out joy, hope, and peace.

One definition of self-pity is "a self-indulgent dwelling on one's own sorrows or misfortunes." Did you catch that? *Self-indulgent dwelling.*

That means you don't just acknowledge the pain—you dwell in it.

You camp there. You rehearse it. You let it name you. And before you know it, you've moved from healthy processing to hopelessness and despair.

Self-pity convinces you that you're powerless.

It whispers that things will never get better.

That hope is foolish.

That you're alone.

That trying again isn't worth it.

It breeds bitterness and isolation.

It keeps you from trusting, healing, and moving forward.

Worst of all—it robs you of the abundant life God created you for.

But hear this, dear one:

You are meant for more.

But...abundance isn't about perfection

If you've believed that living abundantly means everything works out... that you'll never be disappointed... that suffering won't touch you—let this truth set you free:

Abundance is not found in perfection.

It's not about having an easy life.

A flourishing soul isn't untouched by pain.

It's a soul rooted in faith and resilience.

A heart that returns to God again and again—especially in the hard places.

Scripture never promises that all things will be good. We live in a broken world. People disappoint. Pain finds us. But that's not the end of the story. *"And we know that in all things God works for the good of those who love Him..."*

Not all things are good. But in God's hands, all things can be *used* for good. Maybe you can't see it yet. Maybe it won't be clear this side of heaven. But one day, it will be. That's His promise.

So here are some tips on how to rise when self-pity tries to pull you under:

Be real with your emotions.

Give yourself space to grieve, to feel, to process. Healing begins with honesty.

Hold onto hope.

Even when the road ahead feels unclear, don't believe this is the end of your story.

Practice gratitude.

Look for glimmers of goodness. Thank God for even the smallest light —it will shift your perspective.

Keep bringing it back to God.

Again and again, cast your cares on Him. He sees you. He's with you. He won't leave you here.

You are not powerless.

You are not forgotten.

And this season of pain? It is not the end of your story.

Take His hand.

Stand back up.

And walk forward—into the abundant life already waiting for you.

DECLARATION

I am not stuck in pain. God is working in my story. I choose to rise, release self-pity, and step into His abundance.

Reflection

Where in your life have you been dwelling in self-pity instead of reaching for hope?

What truth from God's Word can you hold onto when you feel stuck or discouraged?

Let Go of
Comparison

Day 48

"Pay careful attention to your own work, for then you will get the satisfaction of a job well done, and you won't need to compare yourself to anyone else."
Galatians 6:4 (NLT)

"*COMPARISON IS THE THIEF OF JOY.*" Theodore Roosevelt

How often do you catch yourself comparing your life to someone else's?

In a world flooded with social media and carefully curated highlight reels, it's almost second nature.

Scroll for five minutes, and you'll see perfectly styled homes, dream vacations, and people who seem to have it all together—flawless careers, thriving families, beautiful friendships, and fit bodies.

And where does that leave you?

If you're anything like most of us, it leaves you feeling behind.

As if your life is lacking. As if you're somehow not enough.

But here's the truth:

Comparison is a joy-stealer.

It creeps in quietly, draining your peace, your gratitude, and your sense of purpose.

It distracts you from the life God has uniquely and lovingly given you.

Jesus said,

"The thief comes only to steal and kill and destroy. I came that they may have life and have it abundantly." John 10:10 (ESV)

Comparison shifts your focus away from what you have to what you think you're missing.

It moves your eyes from God's faithfulness to someone else's story.

It trades contentment for envy... and peace for insecurity.

But that's not your story.

You were never meant to live someone else's life.

You were created on purpose, for a purpose—fearfully, wonderfully, and uniquely made in the image of God.

You're not a mistake. You're not a copy. You are a masterpiece.

Think of it this way:

Would you compare a Monet painting to a Michelangelo sculpture and decide one is better?

Of course not. They're completely different—but both breathtaking.

And so are you.

God designed your life to reflect His creativity and goodness.

Jesus came so that you could live *your* abundant life—one marked by peace, purpose, and joy.

So today, when comparison knocks...

Choose something better.

Choose to celebrate.

Choose to be grateful.

Choose to embrace your own journey and the goodness that's already here.

Because you were created to be you.

And that, friend, is more than enough.

DECLARATION

I release the weight of comparison and embrace the beauty of my own story. I am fearfully and wonderfully made—just as I am.

How has comparison affected the way you see yourself or your life?

What are three things you're genuinely grateful for in this current season?

You Don't Have to Please Everyone

Day 49

*"Am I now trying to win the approval of human beings, or of God?
Or am I trying to please people? If I were still trying to please
people, I would not be a servant of Christ."*
Galatians 1:10

ARE you someone who finds it hard to say no?

Do you hold back the truth to avoid disappointing others?

Say "yes" when every part of you is quietly screaming "no"?

Do you stretch yourself thin trying to keep everyone happy—even at your own expense?

If any of that sounds familiar, take a moment and gently ask yourself:

Why am I doing this?

Are you afraid of letting people down?

Do you want others to think well of you?

Do you avoid conflict at all costs?

Have you believed your needs aren't as important as everyone else's?

203

Do you fear being labeled as selfish, difficult, or unkind?

Pleasing people often looks like kindness, but beneath the surface, it's usually rooted in fear—fear of rejection, conflict, or not being enough. Here's the hard truth:

It's exhausting.

When you constantly put others' needs ahead of your own, it doesn't just wear you out—it chips away at your authenticity.

How many times have you agreed to something and later felt anxious, resentful, or overwhelmed?

How often have you smiled and said, *"It's fine,"* when deep down, it wasn't? People-pleasing makes you wear a mask. And wearing that mask every day—hiding your needs, pretending everything's okay when it's not—leads to burnout, bitterness, and shallow relationships. But hear this, friend: **You matter too.**

Your needs, your energy, your peace, and your voice are just as important as anyone else's.

Saying "no" doesn't make you unkind.

It makes you honest.

And honesty is what real connection is built on.

Setting boundaries isn't selfish—it's healthy.

It's a vital part of living with intention and integrity.

Living abundantly means showing up as your whole self.

It means:

Giving from a heart of joy, not guilt or obligation.

Loving others without abandoning yourself.

Trusting that true friends love you for who you are—not for what you do for them. And yes—some people won't like your boundaries. That's okay. Their discomfort doesn't determine your worth. You can't control how others respond, but you *can* choose whether you keep sacrificing your well-being just to keep the peace. And when you step out of people-pleasing and into authenticity, something beautiful happens—

You begin to experience real joy. Real peace. Real relationships rooted in honesty and mutual respect.

So take a deep breath.

Give yourself permission to say no when you need to.

Honor your voice.

And remember—you are just as worthy of love and care as the people you so freely give it to.

DECLARATION

I release the need to please everyone. I honor my voice, trust God's guidance, and love others without losing myself.

Reflection

When was the last time you said "yes" when you truly wanted to say "no"? Why?

What are you afraid might happen if you disappoint someone?

Uproot Self-Doubt
Day 50

"For I know the plans I have for you," declares the Lord, "plans for welfare and not for evil, to give you a future and a hope."
Jeremiah 29:11 (ESV)

SWEET FRIEND, by now we've talked a lot about identity, fear, and the lies that hold you back. Today, consider this a reminder—a return to truth you've already begun to plant deep in your soul.

Because even as you grow, self-doubt has a way of creeping back in.

I see the places where uncertainty still lingers—where fear whispers *you're not enough*, where you hesitate instead of moving forward, and where you wonder if you're really ready for what God is calling you into.

That weight you feel? That inner resistance? That old, familiar critic? You're not alone in it.

But here's the truth we've been repeating on this journey—because it bears repeating again:

You are more than enough.

You are exactly who God created you to be, with everything you need already inside you to walk in the purpose He's set before you.

Self-doubt is a nasty weed that threatens your beautiful soul-garden—like dandelions in a green lawn. You need to keep pulling that weed over and over, and replace it with the seeds of truth.

I know what it's like to feel stuck in the same old loop of fear and second-guessing. To play it safe, settle for less, or wait for "someday." But real growth happens when we choose courage in the face of uncertainty—when we trust God more than we trust our fear.

You don't have to do this alone.

God is with you—not just cheering you on, but walking right beside you, equipping you for every step.

So let this be a sacred pause—a check-in on your journey.

What have you been holding back from lately?

A conversation? A boundary? A dream still waiting on the shelf?

Whatever it is, it's not too late.

It still matters. And so do you.

You were made for boldness.

For peace.

For purpose.

So today, return to what you already know:

You are loved.

You are ready.

You are not alone.

Keep going. Keep believing. And never forget—you are already enough.

DECLARATION

I release self-doubt and root myself in God's truth. I am equipped, loved, and ready to walk boldly in my purpose.

Reflection

Where has self-doubt been creeping back in?

What's one small step you can take this week to uproot it and step forward in faith?

Your Purpose Is Worth the Risk

Day 51

"For God has not given us a spirit of fear, but of power and of love and of a sound mind."
2 Timothy 1:7 (NKJV)

MAY 1, 2007, is a day I'll never forget. What started as a routine six-month follow-up for two benign lumps in my right breast quickly turned into something far more terrifying.

A mammogram.

An ultrasound.

A core biopsy.

And then came the moment I lay on a table in a dark, sterile room—flat on my back, tears rolling down my cheeks. In my spirit, I just knew. Something was deeply wrong. My life was suddenly in question.

Fear wrapped itself around me like a vice, tightening with every *what if* racing through my mind.

What if I had cancer?

What if I died?

What about my young daughters? My husband? My parents?

What about the dreams I hadn't yet lived out?

I remember pleading with God:

"Please don't take me home yet. I haven't done enough for You."

And while I *did* have cancer... cancer never had me.

By God's grace, I was given 15 more years—and counting.

And I am so, so grateful.

But more than grateful, I'm awake.

Awake to how fragile life is. How quickly everything can change.

How none of us are promised tomorrow.

For me, cancer was a wake-up call—a holy reckoning. It forced me to face a painful truth:

I didn't want to reach the end of my life and realize I had let fear keep me small.

I didn't want to play it safe when God had given me so much to give.

That realization shifted everything.

It gave me the courage to:

Launch my life coaching business in 2017—even when fear whispered I'd fail.

Write and publish two books—even when I questioned whether I was a "real" writer.

Show up and offer encouragement in my Facebook community—even when it felt raw and vulnerable.

Because here's the truth I've come to believe deep in my bones:

I would rather fail in pursuit of my purpose than live safely and never try.

I don't want to leave anything on the table.

And I don't want you to either.

Your life is a gift from God.

What you do with it is your gift back to Him.

So stop letting fear win.

Live boldly, love freely, and walk courageously into the life God created you for—before it's too late.

DECLARATION

I will not let fear keep me small. I choose to live boldly, love freely, and trust God with every step of my purpose.

Reflection

Where in your life have you been playing small to stay safe?

What's one small but courageous action you can take this week toward your calling?

Overcome Anxiety by Releasing Control

Day 52

"Cast all your anxiety on Him because He cares for you."
1 Peter 5:7

HEART POUNDING. Mind racing. A flood of worst-case scenarios crashing through your thoughts.

That's how anxiety often shows up—loud, fast, and overwhelming.

For many of us, anxiety grows from one core root: trying to control the uncontrollable. Gripping tightly to *what-ifs* convinces us that disaster is just around the corner. I know the feeling well.

For years, one of my biggest anxiety battles was the fear of flying. Each time I boarded a plane, I was convinced it would crash. I braced myself before we even took off. Every bump, every noise, every unexpected jolt would send my mind spiraling.

Why? Because I wasn't in control. I couldn't fly the plane. I couldn't calm the winds. I couldn't prevent a mechanical failure. And that terrified me. But on one especially anxious flight, something shifted.

I realized I had a choice:

I could white-knuckle my way through the flight, gripped by fear... Or I could take a deep breath, loosen my grip, and choose to trust the pilot. Either way, the outcome wasn't in my hands. But how I experienced the journey was.

Anxiety is a weed—sneaky and persistent. It chokes out peace and tries to overrun the garden of your soul. If left unchecked, it spreads. But like all weeds, it can be pulled up—and replaced with seeds of trust.

Anxiety says, *"If I think hard enough, plan well enough, or anticipate everything, I can avoid pain."*

But life, like flying, is unpredictable.

There will be turbulence.

There will be moments that shake you.

Still—**you were never meant to be in control.**

You were never meant to carry the weight of the world on your shoulders.

When anxiety rises up, don't try to manage it on your own. Take it straight to the Gardener. Lay it at God's feet—every fear, every what-if, every frantic thought. He is in control, so you don't have to be.

Picture your soul as a flourishing garden—peaceful, tended, full of beauty and life. Does anxiety belong there?

No.

Because fear and peace can't thrive in the same soil.

God never promised a life without storms. But He *did* promise to be with you in every one.

I no longer fear flying—not because I gained control, but because I finally surrendered the illusion that I needed it. And life is no different.

You can white-knuckle your way through...

Or you can trust the Pilot and enjoy the ride.

Today, choose trust.

And keep pulling up the weeds that try to steal your peace.

DECLARATION

I release what I cannot control and trust the One who holds it all.
God is my peace, and He is guiding the journey.

In what situation have you been "white-knuckling" through it instead of releasing it to God?

What would it look like today to loosen your grip and trust the Pilot?

BREAK FREE FROM WORRY

DAY 53

*"Therefore do not worry about tomorrow, for tomorrow will worry
about itself. Each day has enough trouble of its own."*
Matthew 6:34

WORRY IS a weed many of us wrestle with daily. For some, it almost
feels natural. I grew up watching my dad worry about everything. He'd
call it "being prepared for the worst," but most of what he feared never
came to pass.

There's a difference between wise planning and being consumed by
anxious thoughts. Worry takes you into an unknown future—and it
never takes God with you. It paints pictures of overwhelming situations
where you're alone, helpless, and unprepared.

But here's what I've learned: worry is a liar and a thief.

It whispers that your worst fears are inevitable, draining your peace and
energy before anything even happens. It convinces you you won't be
able to handle what's coming—and in your fearful imagination, you're
always facing it alone.

But the truth? You are never alone. And you never will be.

Worry is like a fast-growing weed in the garden of your soul. It crowds out peace, robs the nutrients from your joy, and blocks the light of truth. And like any persistent weed, it needs to be pulled—again and again.

I've found the only way to uproot worry is to anchor myself in truth.

The truth is, I don't know the future—but God does.

The truth is, just because I think something doesn't make it real.

The truth is, worry doesn't prepare me—it weakens me.

The truth is, God will be with me in every tomorrow. Nothing will take Him by surprise.

The truth is, I will never face anything alone. Ever.

Worry tempts us to dwell on what-ifs, looping through dread and disaster in our minds. It tricks us into thinking that if we mentally prepare for every worst-case scenario, we'll somehow be safer. But that's a lie. The more we worry, the more our hearts and bodies act like the danger is already here—leaving us exhausted, anxious, and drained.

And still, nothing changes.

Jesus understood the cost of worry. That's why He spoke directly to it:

"Who of you by worrying can add a single hour to your life?" (Luke 12:25) He wasn't minimizing our pain. He was pointing us toward peace. Worrying about tomorrow doesn't help you today. It only robs you of the strength you need for this moment.

So the next time worry creeps in, pulling at your peace like an invasive weed, pause and remember:

God is already in your future.

He's not surprised by anything that's coming.

You are never alone.

You don't need to figure everything out.

You just need to trust Him—for this moment, this step, this day.

Worry is a heavy burden to carry. But you don't have to carry it anymore.

Hand it over to the One who holds it all—your past, your present, and your future.

And rest in the deep peace that only He can give.

DECLARATION

I choose to release worry and trust God with what I cannot control. He is with me now and will be with me in every tomorrow.

Reflection

How does worry affect your energy, joy, or relationships?

What truth about God's character do you need to hold onto right now?

Stop Dwelling on Yesterday

Day 54

*"Forget the former things; do not dwell on the past. See, I am
doing a new thing!"*
Isaiah 43:18–19

How many mornings have you woken up with the weight of
yesterday still pressing on your chest?

How often does your first thought replay what went wrong—the words
you wish you hadn't said, the opportunity you missed, the mistake you
can't undo?

If the answer is *too many times to count,* you're not alone. But here's the
truth: dwelling on yesterday doesn't change it.

It doesn't fix what went wrong.

It doesn't heal what's already happened.

What it *does* is cast a shadow over today.

Instead of letting one hard day pass, you drag it into the next. And then
the next. Before you know it, a single regret begins to spread like a

creeping vine—twisting itself around your joy, your energy, and your peace.

Dwelling on the past is a weed in your soul garden. It chokes new growth. It crowds out fresh hope. It blocks the light.

Picture your mind as a garden.

At the gate stands regret and worry, pounding to be let in. They bring anxiety, shame, and fear—ready to overrun the place meant for peace. But faith is there too—quiet and steady—waiting to be invited. Faith brings beauty instead of burden. It plants seeds of possibility, waters resilience, and gently whispers:

You are not stuck. You are not defined by what happened. There is still more ahead.

And here's the truth:

You get to choose what takes root.

You can't go back and change yesterday. But you *can* choose how you show up today.

You can pull the weeds of regret and clear space for something new to grow.

It won't always be easy. Some thoughts may sneak back in like stubborn crabgrass. Old pain might pop up like dandelions—uninvited, but familiar. But you are not powerless. You are not without tools. And you are not alone.

When you stop feeding old regrets...

When you invite faith in and let go of what was...

You make room for peace.

You begin to wake up lighter.

You start to face each day with courage, not dread.

You see open paths where there once were dead ends.

Because when faith takes root, your soul begins to flourish. And through it all, God is gently reminding you:

"See, I am doing a new thing."

DECLARATION

I release worry and make room for faith to flourish. Today is a new day, and I choose peace over regret.

Reflection

What thought or regret from yesterday have you been holding onto that needs to be released?

What does it look like to invite faith to take root in your heart today?

Release Overwhelm

Day 55

Do not despise these small beginnings, for the Lord rejoices to see the work begin."
Zechariah 4:10 (NLT)

Overwhelm is a weed that quietly creeps into your soul garden, tangling your thoughts and choking your momentum.

You start with a vision—financial freedom, a peaceful home, a restored relationship, better health, a growing business, or a fresh start. You picture it vividly, and for a brief moment, you feel inspired. But then reality hits. You see the mountain standing between where you are and where you want to be.

The debt feels too deep.

The clutter is overwhelming.

The healing seems too far off.

The job search feels endless.

The change you long for feels impossible.

And just like that, inspiration fades.

Overwhelm sets in.

You freeze—not because you don't care, but because you don't know where to begin. That's where the weeds start to grow—whispers of *"It's too much,"* or *"Why bother?"* But this is exactly where you take back your garden—one small step at a time.

Transformation doesn't usually come in sweeping moments. It comes through tiny, faithful steps that may feel insignificant—but are laying down roots of change. The progress may be slow. But slow growth is still growth. And with every step, you're loosening the grip of over-whelm and clearing space for clarity, purpose, and peace.

So instead of letting the mountain stop you, ask:

What's one small step I can take today?

Maybe it's setting a budget.

Maybe it's clearing one drawer.

Maybe it's sending a text, drinking more water, updating your resume, or walking for ten minutes.

Whatever the step—take it. Each time you act, you're pulling up a weed of doubt or delay and planting a seed of intention. Keep going, even when progress feels slow. Hold your *why* close. Remind yourself what matters. What will it feel like to walk into a clutter-free space?

To mend that relationship?

To cross the finish line, step into freedom, or live the life you've dreamed of?

Let that vision be your sunlight. Let it draw you forward. And remember—anything that blocks your growth, whether distraction, discouragement, or fear, can be gently but firmly removed.

God rejoices in your small beginnings.

He sees every step, every effort, every weed you pull out in faith.

So keep tending your soul garden.

One moment.

One decision.

One faithful step at a time.

And one day, you'll look back and realize:

That mountain is no longer in front of you.

It's behind.

DECLARATION

I release overwhelm and choose to move forward—one small step at a time. God is with me in every beginning, and He delights in my progress.

Reflection

What mountain in your life currently feels overwhelming?

What is one small step you can take today toward that goal?

Find Peace in an Imperfect World

Day 56

I have told you these things, so that in Me you may have peace. In this world you will have trouble. But take heart! I have overcome the world."
John 16:33

LIFE WILL NEVER BE PERFECT. Disappointments come. People let you down. You let yourself down. Loved ones leave, conflict flares, mistakes happen, and circumstances blindside you. Sometimes your body doesn't cooperate, your energy runs out, and your best-laid plans fall apart. You can try to manage it all—organize, control, prepare, plan. But life, in all its unpredictability, has a way of shaking even the most careful strategy.

And yet... we still expect perfection.

We still believe that if we just work hard enough, try hard enough, do *everything right*, life will finally feel calm, steady, and safe. But those expectations? That longing for perfection? They're weeds in your soul garden. They take up space that was meant for peace, joy, and trust. Left unchecked, they twist your heart into knots of frustration and discouragement.

So how do you really live—*fully*—in the midst of a world that's flawed, fragile, and fleeting?

You look to Jesus.

HOW DID JESUS LIVE IN AN IMPERFECT WORLD?

The Gospels never portray an easy life. Jesus faced rejection, betrayal, loss, exhaustion, suffering, and pressure.

Yet, He remained loving.

He stayed grounded.

He lived with purpose, peace, and compassion.

How?

He stayed close to the Father.

He didn't pretend things were fine when they weren't.

He set boundaries with people who tried to control Him.

He rested—even in the middle of a storm.

He wept when He grieved.

He prayed often.

He invested in deep, meaningful relationships.

And He kept the long view—He endured pain for the joy set before Him (Hebrews 12:2). He never let the brokenness around Him uproot the truth within Him. And neither should you.

When life is hard, you're not expected to plaster on a smile or pretend everything's okay. Jesus didn't. You're invited to feel it—to grieve, to cry, to be honest. But you're also invited to pull out the weeds of perfection and unrealistic expectations that keep telling you peace depends on your circumstances. Peace doesn't come from control, ease, or everything going your way. Peace is what Jesus *plants* in you when you stay close to Him.

This world is messy, but God's plan for you is still unfolding—and it's beautiful. Hope isn't found in having a pain-free life. Hope is found in Christ, whose love never fails—even when life does.

So today, give yourself permission to release what isn't yours to fix. Let go of the lie that you have to hold everything together. Pull up the weeds of perfection and control.

And tend your soul with truth:

You are not alone. You are not forgotten. You are deeply, unshakably loved.

And the best part?

The best is still to come.

DECLARATION

Even in a broken world, I can live with peace and purpose. My hope is in Christ, and His love sustains me every step of the way.

Reflection

What recent disappointment or hardship is tempting you to lose hope?

Which part of Jesus' example do you need to embrace right now in your own imperfect circumstances?

PART FIVE
FLOURISH IN ALL SEASONS AND LEAVE A LEGACY

A truly abundant garden doesn't bloom for just one season—it flourishes year after year, adapting, deepening, and bearing fruit through every stage of life.

As you've tended the soil of your soul—pulling weeds, planting truth, and nurturing growth—something beautiful has begun to take root. These small, faithful choices you've made are not just transforming your present; they're shaping your future.

This final section invites you to walk in God's sustaining grace—grace that carries you through every change, every challenge, and every new season. Even when circumstances shift, your roots can remain strong and steady in Him.

Flourishing isn't about having a perfect life. It's about living with peace, purpose, and fruitfulness—right where you are, in every season.

And as you live with intention and keep showing up in faith, your life becomes something more than a moment of growth—it becomes a legacy. A garden that blesses others long after you've planted the seeds.

So keep tending. Keep trusting. And get ready to flourish, not just for a season, but for a lifetime.

Love That Leaves a Legacy

Day 57

"...And I pray that you, being rooted and established in love, may have power... to grasp how wide and long and high and deep is the love of Christ."
Ephesians 3:17–18

EARLIER IN THIS JOURNEY, we reflected on the truth that God's love is not something you earn—it's something you receive. And today, we return to that sacred truth with deeper intention. Because this isn't just a comforting idea—it's the foundation of your *legacy*.

The degree to which you receive God's love will shape the legacy you leave.

Why? Because everything flows from it. When you live as someone *deeply loved*, it changes the way you show up in the world. You're no longer trying to prove your worth—you're walking in it. You stop striving and start serving from a place of joy, not pressure. You offer grace to others because you've finally received it for yourself.

When you're rooted in love, you live with more courage. You're not held back by fear of failure or comparison. You speak up. You show up. You give generously—not to earn approval, but to reflect the heart of the One who loves you.

This is how legacy is built—not through grand achievements, but through a life fully received and faithfully poured out. And it all begins with *receiving* God's love as truth—not just intellectually, but experientially.

Let it go beyond a verse you've read or a concept you agree with. Let it become the soil your identity grows in. When His love becomes the lens through which you see yourself, you begin to live from security rather than scarcity.

You lead from compassion instead of control.

You love without fear.

And that love leaves a mark—not just in this moment, but for generations.

So pause and come back to this truth:

You are already loved.

Fully. Freely. Unconditionally.

You don't have to earn it. You simply receive it.

And when you do, **your life becomes a living legacy of His love.**

DECLARATION

I receive God's love as the truth that defines me. His love shapes how I live, give, and love—and becomes the legacy I leave behind.

Reflection

How has your willingness—or resistance—to receive God's love shaped the way you show up in your life?

What shifts when you begin to see your legacy as something built on being loved, not just doing more?

Nurture Yourself to Love Others Well

Day 58

"Love your neighbor as yourself. There is no commandment greater than these."
Mark 12:31

You've likely heard the command: *"Love your neighbor as yourself."* But have you ever paused to reflect on what that really means? It assumes you know how to love yourself first.

If you overlook your own well-being while constantly giving to others, love can start to feel heavy—like a duty instead of a joy. Without rhythms of rest and renewal, your patience wears thin, your compassion fades, and your joy begins to wilt.

True love grows from a well-tended soul.

It's not selfish to care for yourself—it's essential.

When you nourish your heart with God's truth, set healthy boundaries, and receive His love regularly, you create the conditions for real, lasting love to take root. Think of the fruit of the Spirit—love, joy, peace, patience, kindness, goodness, faithfulness, gentleness, and self-control.

These aren't random character traits. They're the *fruit* of a life connected to the Vine. When your soul is neglected, those qualities struggle to grow. But when your heart is nourished, they blossom naturally.

Jesus modeled this beautifully. He withdrew to quiet places, honored His need for rest, expressed emotion, and stayed deeply connected to the Father. If Jesus needed space to renew His spirit, so do we.

Self-care is not a distraction from love—it's preparation for it. It's how you build the strength and presence to show up fully for those God has placed in your life.

So today, choose to care for yourself—not from pride, but from wisdom.

When you do, love becomes something you can offer freely, with joy— and that kind of love leaves a legacy.

Here is quick reminder of five essential soul-nurturing practices to help you flourish in love:

1. **Speak kindly to yourself.** Your inner voice matters. If you wouldn't say it to someone you love, don't say it to yourself. Use words that build up, not tear down.
2. **Let go of perfection.** You were never meant to be flawless— only faithful. God's grace is more than enough. Extend it to yourself daily.
3. **Set healthy boundaries.** Boundaries don't push people away —they create space for connection, rest, and balance.
4. **Remember who you are.** Your value doesn't depend on performance. You are deeply loved, fully known, and created with purpose.
5. **Stay rooted in God's love.** Your soul needs regular nourishment. Scripture, prayer, and stillness keep you grounded and growing.

So as you care for your soul with intention, remember: nurturing yourself isn't just for your sake—it's how you grow a life of love that blesses others and leaves a lasting impact.

DECLARATION

I receive God's love and care for myself with grace so I can love others well.

Reflection

Where might you need to set a boundary to protect your emotional and spiritual well-being?

How could loving yourself more intentionally help you flourish and deepen your relationships with others?

What Will You Leave
Behind in Others?
Day 59

"Each of you should use whatever gift you have received to serve others, as faithful stewards of God's grace in its various forms."
1 Peter 4:10

ONE EVENING, a line from a song caught my ear— *"I want to be known by love."* It repeated again and again, and with it came a gentle whisper from the Holy Spirit: *"Your legacy matters."* That phrase has stayed with me ever since.

Whether you realize it or not, you're creating a legacy.

With every word, every act of kindness, every way you choose to show up—you are planting seeds. The question is: *What will those seeds grow into? What are you leaving behind in others?*

After losing both of my parents within three weeks of each other, this became deeply personal. For 59 years, I had the gift of walking through life with them—two people who weren't perfect, but who loved deeply and faithfully. After they passed, my daughter gave me a painting of them from their 65th anniversary. I see it every day. And each time I do, one truth settles in my heart:

Their legacy wasn't found in what they gave *to* me—it was in what they gave *within* me. We often confuse inheritance with legacy. Inheritance is what we leave *for* others—money, possessions, things. But legacy is what we leave *in* others—love, wisdom, presence, and faithfulness. It's the fruit that continues to grow long after we're gone.

My parents didn't come from easy or perfect beginnings. They could have repeated the brokenness of the past. But by God's grace, they chose differently. They used their lives to love well—with their time, their gifts, and their unwavering compassion.

My Father's Legacy: My dad, a social worker and Executive Director of Big Brothers/Big Sisters, used his leadership and empathy to help mend what was broken in others. At church, he made sure no one left without a hug. His quiet warmth made people feel seen.

My Mother's Legacy: My mom raised kids, waitressed, put herself through college in her 40s, and later became an advocate for struggling students. But her greatest impact? The way she made people *feel*. She saw those who were often overlooked—and made them feel like they mattered.

After she passed, I heard stories from waitresses, nurses, and even those who barely spoke English—each one touched by her kindness. And now? I carry her legacy forward every time I pause to truly notice someone who might otherwise be forgotten.

Your Legacy Is Being Written Right Now

Every skill, every lesson, every experience—God wants to use all of it.

Your ability to listen, create, teach, organize, bake, plan, encourage, or lead—none of it is random. These are seeds you've been entrusted with.

You don't need a spotlight to leave a legacy.

You just need a willing heart.

The question isn't *if* you'll leave a legacy.

It's *what kind* you'll leave.

And it's never too late to shape it with grace and intention.

Maybe your season looks different now. Maybe you can't do what you once did. But as I reminded my mom in her later years: *"You're still here to love. The way you love may change, but the world still needs it."*

Friend, the world still needs what only you can give.

DECLARATION

Today, I choose to live with intention—using what God has given me to love well and sow seeds of kindness, faith, and compassion that will bloom long after I'm gone.

Reflection

What legacy did the people who shaped you leave in your life?

What do you want others to remember most about you?

You are Made to Give Freely

Day 60

"Give, and you will receive. Your gift will return to you in full—pressed down, shaken together to make room for more, running over, and poured into your lap."
Luke 6:38 (NLT)

HAVE you ever noticed how giving—your time, your attention, your love—doesn't just bless others but leaves your own heart fuller?

It's one of God's beautiful paradoxes: the more you pour out, the more you are filled.

We sometimes think generosity has to be big—writing a large check, volunteering for a major cause, or making a public sacrifice. But true giving isn't measured by size.

It's measured by love.

Jesus reminds us that when you give with an open heart, even the smallest offering becomes abundant—pressed down, shaken together, running over.

Small acts matter:

A kind word.
A listening ear.
A handwritten note.
A moment of patience when frustration rises.

Each one is a seed. Each one plants love. Each one leaves something behind.

We live in a world filled with loneliness. Even those who appear "fine" are often carrying unseen heaviness. Maybe you've felt it too. But here's the hope: when you give—when you choose to reflect God's generous heart—you are part of the healing.

You were made to give.

To live connected.

To reflect your Creator by loving in tangible ways.

Mother Teresa once said, *"Not all of us can do great things. But we can do small things with great love."*

That's the heart of a flourishing life.

Small, Spirit-led acts that leave a lasting legacy of love.

Everyday opportunities to give:

> *Preparing a meal with care.*
> *Sending a thoughtful text.*
> *Greeting someone with warmth.*
> *Praying quietly for someone in need.*
> *Listening fully, without distraction.*
> *Saying "thank you" with meaning.*
> *Holding space for a hurting heart.*

These small moments may not make headlines, but they echo in eternity. They shape the kind of legacy that outlives you—one that continues to bless, encourage, and uplift others long after you're gone. Because giving doesn't just help others—it transforms *you*. It deepens your sense of purpose. It connects you to others. And it opens your heart to the joy of living generously.

So today, give—not out of obligation, but out of overflow. Let kindness become your rhythm. Let generosity become part of your legacy.

You were made to give.

And the world needs what only you can offer.

DECLARATION

Today, I choose to give freely—trusting that every act of love I share creates light, hope, and connection in the world.

Reflection

In what areas of your life have you felt most fulfilled through giving?

Are there any fears or barriers that hold you back from giving freely—such as time, energy, or vulnerability?

Be the Answer to Someone's Prayer

Day 61

"Therefore, as God's chosen people, holy and dearly loved, clothe yourselves with compassion, kindness, humility, gentleness and patience."
Colossians 3:12

"Small acts of love create waves of hope." Author unknown

HAVE you ever stopped to wonder if you might be the answer to someone's prayer?

All around you—family, friends, neighbors, strangers—are people carrying invisible burdens.

Some are grieving.

Some are lonely.

Some are simply asking God for a sign that they're not forgotten.

And here's the beautiful truth: God often answers prayers through people, through *you*.

Being an answer to someone's prayer doesn't require anything grand—it simply requires a willingness to *see*.

To pause.

To look up from your routine and notice who around you might need a moment of compassion.

Who's feeling worn out?

Who seems distant or discouraged?

Who might just need to know they are seen and loved?

Sometimes the need is clear—a friend facing illness or loss.

Other times, it's more subtle—the tired smile, the silence in a conversation, the person who quietly pulls away.

Compassion begins with awareness and the willingness to take even a small action.

You don't have to do something huge to make a difference.

The smallest seed of love—planted in faith—can grow into something eternal.

A sincere smile.

A handwritten note.

A text that simply says, *"You're on my heart today."*

A whispered prayer on someone's behalf.

A quiet moment of presence and listening.

These are the simple acts that light the path for someone else.

These are the moments that build legacy—not in things, but in *people*.

Love has a ripple effect.

One small act of kindness can touch a heart... and then another... and then another.

You may never see the full impact of your actions—but God does.

Your Life Is a Vessel of God's Love

God has given you gifts, time, and a heart capable of reflecting His love.

You don't have to be perfect.

You just have to be willing.

Willing to notice.

Willing to respond.

Willing to plant seeds of hope in ordinary moments.

So today, live with intention.

Let love guide your decisions.

Let compassion shape your interactions.

Because when you live like this, you don't just leave a mark—you leave a legacy.

And your legacy becomes the answer to prayers you may never hear... but heaven surely does.

DECLARATION

Today, I choose to notice and respond with love. Even the smallest act can be an answer to someone's prayer.

Reflection

When has someone been an answer to your own prayer?

Who around you might be silently praying for help, comfort, or encouragement today? Ask God to show you.

Legacy in the Little Moments

Day 62

"In everything, set them an example by doing what is good."
Titus 2:7

MY SWEET TWO-YEAR-OLD grandson is in the phase where he copies everything—my words, my tone, even how I fold my hands when I pray.

It's both precious and sobering.

Because in those small, ordinary moments, I'm reminded: *they're watching.*

The next generation is watching how we live.

How we speak.

How we handle disappointment, stress, and joy.

How we show kindness to others.

How we pray, forgive, and respond when no one else is looking.

And all of it is planting seeds.

Seeds of compassion, courage, faith, and character.

Legacy isn't just what we leave behind someday—it's what we're shaping right now, in the daily choices we make and the presence we offer.

We don't have to be perfect.

But we *do* have to be present.

More than anything, I want my grandson to remember that he was deeply loved. That God was real and near. That his Grammy walked in grace, lived with purpose, and pointed to Jesus in the way she lived.

You carry that same power.

Your influence—whether you're a parent, grandparent, mentor, or friend—is shaping lives in ways you may never fully see. And it's often in the quiet, unseen moments that the greatest impact takes root.

So today, pause and ask yourself:

What kind of life are you modeling?

What seeds are you sowing into the hearts around you?

Let it be one of love, faithfulness, and quiet strength.

Because a life well lived is the most beautiful legacy of all.

DECLARATION

I choose to live with love, purpose, and grace—trusting that my daily actions are planting a legacy that honors God and blesses others.

Reflection

Who in your life is watching and learning from how you live? What seeds are you sowing into their heart?

What simple habits or actions can you practice consistently to reflect your faith and values in everyday life?

Loving Your Friends Through Prayer

Day 63

"Carry each other's burdens, and in this way you will fulfill the law of Christ."
Galatians 6:2

You never really know what someone is going through behind the scenes.

Even the strongest, most put-together friends can be silently carrying deep grief, anxiety, discouragement, or fear. Smiles can mask struggle. Busyness can hide pain. And sometimes, the ones who give the most are the ones who need prayer the most.

That's why lifting your friends in prayer is such a sacred gift.

Even if they haven't shared a word, even if you don't know the full story —your prayers matter. They carry love. They carry comfort. They carry power.

When you pray for your friends, you step into a quiet ministry of presence. You stand in the gap when their faith feels weak. You bring their needs before the One who knows them fully and loves them completely.

This is part of your legacy: being the kind of person who holds space for others, even in silence.

Your prayers may never be seen or heard by the world, but heaven hears every one. And they leave an imprint on the lives of those you love.

So don't underestimate the ripple effect of a whispered prayer.

God may be prompting you to pray today for someone who hasn't yet said a word—but desperately needs to feel seen and supported.

Simple ways to love your friends well through prayer:

Ask God to place a specific friend on your heart today.

Send a message that simply says, "*I prayed for you today.*"

Write their name in your journal and pray for peace, strength, and joy.

Trust that your quiet intercession matters—more than you may ever know.

DECLARATION

I will quietly carry my friends in prayer, trusting that unseen love creates eternal impact.

Reflection

Who in your life might be silently carrying something heavy?

How can you quietly show up for them through prayer or presence this week?

Keep Planting Seeds of Love

Day 64

"So neither the one who plants nor the one who waters is anything, but only God, who makes things grow."
1 Corinthians 3:7

"Even when you can't see it, your love is taking root." Anonymous

Have you ever poured your heart into someone—offering wisdom, encouragement, or truth—only to be met with silence, resistance, or indifference?

Maybe it's your child, your spouse, a friend, or someone you mentor.

You know what you're offering is good, but they just can't (or won't) receive it.

It's frustrating, even heartbreaking.

But here's the truth that brings peace:

You can't force a seed to grow. But you can plant it.

And in God's hands, that seed holds immeasurable potential.

Seeds don't sprout overnight.

They often lie hidden—dormant beneath the surface—for days, months, or even years before signs of growth appear.

But even in the silence, God is at work.

A gentle word.

A patient response.

A small act of grace when frustration rises.

These are the seeds of love, humility, and hope. They are not wasted.

Think about your own life—how many truths took time to take root?

How often did a lesson or encouragement from someone in your past come back to you just when you needed it? That's the quiet power of a planted seed.

It's tempting to give up when you don't see progress. But spiritual growth is God's job, not yours.

Your calling is to **keep planting**—with love, with prayer, with trust.

To water what you can, and surrender what you can't control.

This is how you build a legacy.

Not by fixing others, but by faithfully planting truth in love and letting God bring the increase.

So don't lose heart.

Keep showing up.

Keep speaking life.

Keep praying when it feels like nothing's changing.

Because one day, in God's perfect timing, those buried seeds will break through the soil and bloom in ways you never imagined.

And when they do, you'll know:

It wasn't in vain.

It was love, planted in faith—and God made it grow.

DECLARATION

I will keep planting seeds of love, grace, and truth—trusting that God is working beneath the surface in His perfect timing.

Are you feeling discouraged by a lack of visible progress in someone you love?

What is one small "seed" you can plant today—through a word, prayer, or action?

Daily Choices Ripple into Eternity
Day 65

"Let us not become weary in doing good, for at the proper time we will reap a harvest if we do not give up."
Galatians 6:9

"Every decision is a seed planted in the garden of your future."
Anonymous

EVERY CHOICE YOU MAKE—WHETHER big or small—is shaping the life you're building. What you eat, how you speak, how you spend your time and money, how you respond to stress, how you care for your soul and relationships—*it all matters.*

These daily decisions form habits. Those habits form patterns. And those patterns shape your future—and your legacy. So pause and ask:

What do I want my life to stand for?

What truly matters to me?

The small, seemingly insignificant choices you make today ripple into tomorrow—and beyond. They're not just shaping your present—they're planting seeds that will bear fruit far into the future. Choosing to care for your soul is like putting on a new pair of glasses. You begin to see beauty more clearly—even in broken places.

It doesn't mean you ignore pain or pretend life is perfect. It means you allow hardship to draw you closer to the Source of your strength. It means you choose to live with light—even in a dark world.

When you live with an abundant mindset, your life becomes a beacon. Your presence reflects God's hope, grace, and love. That's the quiet power of a soul tended daily with intention.

So dear friend, keep showing up.

Keep shining your light.

Your choices matter.

Your life matters.

None of us knows how many days we have left.

We rarely wake up thinking, *This could be my last day.*

But life can shift in an instant.

When that moment comes, will you be able to say you truly lived?

That you gave love freely, shared your gifts boldly, and followed the purpose God placed in you?

When I was diagnosed with breast cancer in 2007, I was forced to confront just how fragile life really is.

Suddenly, everything felt more precious—my dreams, my time, my family.

I longed for more days with my husband and young daughters.

I wanted to spare my parents the pain of losing another child.

And deep within, I knew I still had more to give—more love, more light, more purpose.

By God's grace, I'm still here—more than 15 years later.

Losing my sisters, and more recently both of my parents, has only deepened my awareness that time is a gift.

And like any gift, it must be used wisely.

Time is a non-renewable resource.

You don't get it back—but you *do* get to choose how you spend it.

So here's your invitation:

Live with intention.

Make choices that reflect what matters most.

Don't wait for a crisis to wake you up to what you already know deep down.

Start now.

Right here.

In the ordinary, sacred moments of today.

Because how you live today is shaping the story you'll leave behind.

DECLARATION

I choose to live today with eternal purpose—planting seeds of love, grace, and truth that will grow beyond my lifetime.

Reflection

What small daily choices are you making that either support or hinder the life you want to build?

If you knew your time was limited, what would you do differently today?

Your Story Matters

Day 66

"Come and hear, all you who fear God; let me tell you what He has done for me."
Psalm 66:16

"Your story may be just the thing God uses to help someone get through theirs."
Sharon Jaynes

I DEEPLY BELIEVE THIS: **God never wastes our pain.**

What the enemy meant for harm, God can use for good—not just in our own lives, but in the lives of others, too.

Shortly after I was diagnosed with breast cancer, I whispered this simple prayer:

Lord, if I have to go through this, don't let it be wasted. Use it to make me better, stronger—or to help someone else.

And He did.

As I walked through my healing, God kept placing women in my path who were just beginning their cancer journey. I could see the fear in their eyes, hear the tremble in their voices—and I knew.

It wasn't coincidence.

Each one was a divine appointment.

There's a special comfort in being seen by someone who's *been there.* Someone who listens—not just with ears, but with the heart.

Friend, your story—every joy, sorrow, hardship, and breakthrough—has purpose.

The things you've walked through, the prayers you've prayed, the pain you've survived—they're not just part of your past. They're seeds of encouragement waiting to be sown into the life of someone else.

Have you paused to reflect on the quiet ways God has been at work in your life?

How many times has He protected you, redirected you, or healed you in ways you didn't even realize you needed?

There's a thread of grace running through your story—woven through every detour, disappointment, and miracle. Sometimes it's clear in the moment. Often, we only recognize it when we look back.

Take a breath. Let gratitude rise.

Thank Him for His mercy—

For carrying you through the valleys.

For standing between you and danger.

For whispering truth when you were close to giving up.

For the doors He opened... and the ones He lovingly closed.

Your story is a living testimony of His faithfulness.

And it's not over yet.

You are deeply loved by an extraordinary God.

He has carried you, shaped you, and placed you here—for such a time as this.

So walk in confidence.

Live with intention.

And when God prompts you, don't be afraid to share your story.

Because someone out there needs it.

Your words might be the encouragement that gives them strength.

Your testimony might be the light they've been praying for.

When you share your story with grace and humility, you leave behind something that lasts—*a legacy of faith.*

So keep trusting.

Keep believing.

And stay open to the beautiful things still unfolding.

DECLARATION

God is using my story—every joy and struggle—for His glory. I choose to share it with courage, trusting it will bring hope and healing to others.

Reflection

How has God used a difficult season in your life to bring about growth, healing, or a deeper awareness of His grace?

Who in your life might need encouragement from your story, and how can you share it in a way that points them to God's faithfulness?

LIVE THE FLOURISHING LIFE YOU WERE CREATED FOR

DAY 67

"They will be like a tree planted by the water that sends out its roots by the stream. It does not fear when heat comes; its leaves are always green."
Jeremiah 17:8

YOU ARE NOT JUST any seed—you are a masterpiece, intentionally planted by the Master Gardener, your Creator and Designer, in the rich soil of His grace and love.

You are one of a kind.

Your worth isn't measured by what you do, but by Whose you are.

Just as a rose seed carries everything it needs to bloom into a rose bush, you already hold within you the God-given potential to flourish. But growth doesn't happen passively. It takes intention. It takes tending.

As you stay rooted in the love of the Gardener—through prayer, reflection, and communion with His Spirit—you'll find rest, wisdom, mercy, and grace for every challenge.

Daily soul-care practices like journaling, creating margin, setting boundaries, and choosing peace aren't just good habits—they're sacred rhythms that align your life with God's design for abundance.

Still, flourishing doesn't happen by accident.

Weeds of self-doubt, perfectionism, people-pleasing, and fear will try to take over if left unchecked.

You must be intentional about uprooting what no longer serves your growth and replacing it with truth, peace, and purpose.

When life feels heavy, slow down.

Breathe deeply.

Treat your emotions with gentleness.

Ask for help—from God and from people who speak life into your soul.

These small, faithful choices—made day by day—open your heart to the kind of life that's rich in meaning, anchored in grace, and overflowing with love.

Flourishing is not a destination.

It's a way of life.

It's the quiet decision to keep showing up, to keep trusting, and to let God shape something beautiful within you.

If you've walked through these 67 days of soul-care meditations, you've already begun that process—renewing your mind (Romans 12:2), strengthening your spirit, and tending the garden of your heart . If your journey hasn't been perfect or consistent, take heart. You can always begin again. Start where you are. Your soul is worth the investment.

Your nurtured life will bear fruit—not only for your own joy, but for generations to come.

As your roots grow deeper in God's love, your legacy of resilience, grace, and faith will continue to bloom and bless beyond what you can see.

So stay close to the Master Gardener.

Trust His timing.

Keep tending your soul.

You were created to thrive.

And dear one—**keep blooming.**

DECLARATION

I am rooted in God's love, nurtured by His grace, and created to flourish in every season of life.

Reflection

What "weeds" in your life—negative thoughts, habits, or influences—still need to be uprooted?

What rhythms will help you stay grounded and flourishing in God's love moving forward?

A FINAL WORD
FROM MY HEART TO YOURS

Dear Beautiful Soul,

Thank you for taking this journey. Whether you've walked through each day of this devotional or turned to its pages in moments when your heart needed hope, please know this:

You are not the same woman who began.

You've planted seeds.

You've tended your soul.

You've begun the sacred, ongoing journey of flourishing—rooted in grace, truth, and the deep, unfailing love of your Creator.

But friend, this isn't the end. It's the beginning of something new.

If your heart is still longing for deeper healing...

If you're ready to move beyond grief, overwhelm, or confusion...

If you're seeking clarity about who you are and what God is calling you to next...

I want to personally invite you to continue this journey—with me by your side.

I equip and empower Christian women who feel stuck in grief or life transitions to heal their hearts, rediscover their God-given identity, and move forward with peace and purpose.

Whether you're navigating loss, stepping into a new season, or simply wondering where you belong, you don't have to walk it alone.

Coaching with me is more than setting goals—it's about soul care. It's about becoming deeply aligned with the woman God created you to be. Together, we'll gently explore what's been holding you back, tend to the wounds beneath the surface, and create a personalized vision for the flourishing life God wants for you.

If you're part of a women's group or faith-based community, I also offer speaking engagements that weave together biblical wisdom, personal stories, and practical tools for healing and hope. It would be a joy to pour into your group and help others begin their own journey toward wholeness.

So if something in these pages stirred your heart—don't let it fade.

Please reach out. Let's take the next step together.

Keep growing. Keep healing. Keep blooming.

You were made to flourish—and it would be my honor to walk alongside you.

You can learn more or connect with me here:

Visit: www.DrRichelle.com

Email: connect@drrichelle.com

Join my free Facebook community: *Abundant Soul Care with Dr. Richelle*

With deep gratitude and great hope for your journey,

Dr. Richelle, *Abundant Life Coach*

ABOUT THE AUTHOR

Dr. Richelle Hoekstra-Anderson—a clinical psychologist turned Abundant Life Coach—has a heart for the Christian woman in midlife who's feeling stuck, burned out, and stretched too thin. She understands how, after years of pouring into everyone else, it's easy to lose connection with your own heart.

With compassion, wisdom, and unshakable faith, Dr. Richelle helps women slow down, reconnect with who they are in Christ, and step into the abundant life of peace, freedom, and purpose God designed them to live. She weaves together her background in psychology and her love for Scripture to offer practical, grace-filled soul-care tools that help women realign their lives with their true identity and unique God-given design.

Through her coaching, courses, and soul-nourishing resources, she empowers women to move from just getting by to truly flourishing—from survival mode to lives marked by clarity, confidence, and meaningful impact.

At home, her heart belongs to her husband of more than 40 years, their two married daughters and devoted sons-in-law, a treasured grandson (with another expected in September 2025), and two beloved canine companions.

www.ingramcontent.com/pod-product-compliance
Lightning Source LLC
Chambersburg PA
CBHW070909120626
46546CB00001B/200